Does God care about the intimate lives of His  believes that since God made sex possible, ar therefore, advisable to inquire about His pei spective in the Song of Solomon and elsewhere scattered through the Scriptures, Dr. Akin brings to bear on the subject the mind of a fine scholar, the rhetorical excellence of an outstanding preacher, and the remarkable example of a great husband and father. This is the scripturally grounded, exciting, and spiritual book pastors and counselors need for families who desire that even their most intimate moments with each other will be an anthem of praise to our God.

Paige Patterson, President
Southeastern Baptist Theological Seminary
Wake Forest, North Carolina

Dr. Danny Akin has done every marriage a huge favor by writing this much-needed book on a topic that every married couple needs to hear. A sensitive subject is handled with dignity from a biblical perspective but in a lighthearted way that makes for a great read. Dr. Akin has modeled this book in his marriage—now he can mentor the rest of us as well. Husbands and wives—enjoy!

James Merritt, Pastor
First Baptist Church
Snellville, Georgia

Far too long the church has been silent on the subject of sex. Yet as my friend Danny Akin states in his Introduction, "Sex was God's idea." So it's time we addressed sex for what it is—part of God's perfect creation and plan for husband and wife. *God on Sex* is an insightful look at God's design for love, sex, and intimacy within the marriage covenant. From the practical biblical principles set forth in this book, you'll discover the simple yet profound truth—God's way works . . . and it works beautifully!

H. Edwin Young, Pastor
Second Baptist Church
Houston, Texas

Many will be surprised to discover that God is absolutely positive about sex! Dr. Danny Akin clearly and biblically writes a manual for marriage and intimacy from the Song of Songs. In *God on Sex* you will fully discover God's plan and purpose for the gift of love and delight in the joys of wholesome, Christ-honoring romantic relationships.

Jack Graham, Pastor
Prestonwood Baptist Church
Dallas, Texas

God on Sex is the most practical book written on love and marriage in the last decade. This will be required reading at Prestonwood for every couple before they say "I do." God has used Danny Akin in my life throughout my ministry and this book, like Danny, is both practical and inspiring. This motivational work will help you discover the sexual and emotional satisfaction God created you to enjoy. Everyone longs for a great marriage, and *God on Sex* will take you there.

Mike Buster, Executive Pastor
Prestonwood Baptist Church
Dallas, Texas

If you are looking for a book jam-packed with practical insights about love, sex, and marriage, if you want clear biblical teaching brought into everyday life, and if you are ready to laugh hard, weep remorsefully, reflect deeply, and pledge to love in faithfulness and joy, you will find resources for all this and more in Daniel Akin's *God on Sex*. Akin offers an astonishing vision of biblical marriage from one of the most neglected books of the Bible. His personal transparency and choice anecdotes pepper the book. But most of all, his deep passion for true marital love and intimacy, lived out in a complementarian relationship that God designed marriage to be, shines through like a beacon into the fog of our confused culture. Christian husbands and wives alike will learn much, be challenged to apply much, and through this find their marriages renewed and enriched, to the greater glory of God.

Bruce A. Ware, President
Council on Biblical Manhood and Womanhood

Boldly unveiling truth from the Song of Songs, *God on Sex* provides a delightful, insightful journey towards deep marital intimacy. Drawing from real life experiences and incorporating thought-provoking questions and practical suggestions, this biblically based tool will provide encouragement for couples and church leaders desiring godly transformation of marriages.

William R. Cutrer M.D.
Associate Professor of Christian Ministry
Director of Gheens Center for Family Ministry
The Southern Baptist Theological Seminary

Finally, the bold, insightful, mind-stretching principles so often shared in Dr. Danny Akin's seminars have been put into writing. Actually they were there all along, tucked away in the pages of the Bible, where you can find the mind of God on every pertinent subject. Gathering these truths together from the Song of Solomon, Dr. Akin gives us *God on Sex*. And none too soon for a generation that is desperately "looking for love in all the wrong places." This is a book everyone who really cares about love and marriage will want to read.

Tom Elliff, Pastor
First Southern Baptist Church
Del City, Oklahoma
Chairman, Southern Baptist Council on Family Life

Wow, what a book! Romance isn't just for the beginning of a relationship. It can last throughout married life. Dr. Akin explores our society's romantic ideals and how they can apply to your marriage, and he does it from the background of the Word of God. Exposition like this and the accompanying humor and up-to-date surveys allow Akin to balance romance with realism. It also provides answers to help you find new romantic potential in your relationship. He explores the real meaning of love and simply tells us that love is a feeling you feel when you feel that you're going to get a feeling that you never felt before. We commend this book to every married couple as a biblical primer for romance.

Harold and Barbara O'Chester, Directors
Regeneration Retreat Ministry
Austin, Texas

God's plan for marriage includes the bedroom. Daniel Akins' book gives God's perspective on sex, and offers a wonderful resource to help couples enhance the romance in their marriage.

Dennis Rainey, President
FamilyLife

GOD

on SEX

GOD
on Sex

The Creator's Ideas
About Love, Intimacy
and Marriage

DANIEL Akin

BROADMAN
&HOLMAN
PUBLISHERS

NASHVILLE, TENNESSEE

To my wife
Charlotte
who is my darling, my love, and my best friend.
How beautiful you are and how pleasant,
O love, with such delights.

Contents

Eat, friends! Drink! Be intoxicated with love!
SONG OF SONGS 5:1B

Introduction

God's Manual for Sex, Love, Intimacy, and Marriage

Sex was God's idea. Yes, I know it is hard to believe, but God is the one who came up with this fantastic idea, and I believe He was having a really good day when He did! Sex was God's idea, and He gave it to us as a wonderful gift for our *pleasure* and *procreation*. God is pro-sex. He believes in it. He is for it. A study of the Song of Solomon (or Song of Songs) makes this abundantly clear.

Marriage was also God's idea. I believe He was also having a really good day when He gave this gift to us. This gift is intended for *partnership* and *protection*. When sex and marriage are experienced and enjoyed together as God intended, the joys and blessings that are ours are seldom, if ever, surpassed in this life.

So what's the problem? Why is it that so many—too many— marriages end in divorce? Why is it that more and more persons are dissatisfied with their sex life both inside and outside of marriage? I believe the answer is simple: we have forgotten or ignored what God has to say about sex, love, intimacy, and marriage. We have failed to read and heed the Master's Manual for Marriage,

1

and the price many have paid has been high indeed. It can be different if we will do things God's way.

God is so interested in and committed to the intimate, romantic, and sexual aspects of marriage that He gave us an entire book of the Bible dedicated to the subject. It is called the Song of Songs or the Song of Solomon.

When my wife Charlotte and I lived in Wake Forest, North Carolina, we were invited to participate in the Newlywed Game at a Valentine's banquet. Actually, all of the couples participating this particular evening had been married for some time. We had been married about fifteen years ourselves. I am delighted to tell you that we won the evening's event by an overwhelming margin. Two questions in particular were decisive in our victory.

First, Charlotte had been asked to name the last thing I had fixed at our home. Now, you need to understand, I had a "mechanical bypass" performed at birth! I struggle to change a lightbulb without burning my finger or shocking myself. I was absolutely blank in trying to come up with anything. Finally, out of time and in desperation, I said, "Can you say NOTHING!" The crowd exploded in applause as Charlotte held up a card that said "NOTHING!"

Second, the wives were asked, "What is your husband's favorite book of the Bible?" Well, all the other couples missed it. One wife said "John," but her husband said "Romans." Another wife said "Philippians," but her husband said "1 John." When it came my turn, I must confess I was a bit haughty. I said, "Folks this isn't fair. I'm certain that on that card in my wife's lap is written 'The Song of Solomon!'" This time the crowd went nuts as Charlotte held up the answer she had written: "The Song of Solomon."

Why do I love this book so much? What is its attraction? It is because this side of heaven, outside of having a personal relationship with Jesus Christ, the Son of God, I believe the best thing going is marriage and family. When we do marriage and family God's way, it is great. It is awesome. It is wonderful. The Song of Songs teaches us how to do it God's way, and it leaves nothing out. A beautiful love song, it portrays the deep, genuine love that a man and woman should enjoy in marriage. It teaches us that a successful marriage requires commitment and involves work, but that it is worth every investment we make. The book celebrates the joys of physical, intimate, sexual love. Sex is good; it is God's gift. It should be enjoyed and enjoyed often. This good gift of God will find its fullest expression realized when a man and woman give themselves completely to each other in the marriage relationship.

God knows nothing of casual sex, because in reality there is no such thing. What is often called casual sex is always costly. Sexually transmitted diseases (STDs), unexpected pregnancy, and psychological and spiritual scars are some of the results, and the price paid, because we have approached God's good gift of sex all too casually. Sexual attraction is inevitable. It is what God intended. However, unless we follow God's plan, we will miss out on His best and suffer the painful and tragic consequences in the process.

The Song of Songs explains the purpose and place of sex as God designed it. When we make love the way God planned, we enjoy the security of a committed relationship, experience the joy of unreserved passion, and discover the courage to give ourselves completely to another in unhindered abandonment.

Sociologists and marriage and family counselors are now discovering that the most emotionally and physically satisfying sex is between committed married partners, and that satisfaction from sex increases with sexual exclusivity (one partner only), emotional investment in the relationship, and a lasting horizon for the marriage. They are also discovering that marriage is an excellent tonic for both mental and physical health, and that marriage slam dunks cohabitation in both areas.[1]

And what about our children? A culture awash in divorce and cohabitation can no longer deny the flood of data that tells it like it is. In 1997, the number of unmarried couples in the U.S. topped four million, up from less than half a million in 1960. Today "only 42% of 14–18 year olds live with their married mother and father. In Wisconsin, children of divorce are 12 times more likely to be jailed than kids in a 2-parent family and those living with never-married single parents are 22 times more at risk." In the highly acclaimed report, *The Effects of Divorce on America,* Patrick Fagan and Robert Rector point out that "a child living with a single mother is 14 times more likely to suffer serious physical abuse than those in intact two-parent families, twice as likely to drop out of school, three times as likely to get pregnant as a teenager, and far more likely to commit suicide."[2] Katherine Kersten puts it on the line when she writes, "What is the No. 1 public health threat to American children? . . . Could it be smoking? . . . How about child abuse? . . . Maybe drugs? . . . The greatest health threat to American children is none of these. It is something we, as parents, bring on our children ourselves: divorce."[3]

I do not share these sobering truths to shame but to inspire and motivate. Nor is it my goal to throw rocks at anyone. We would all change the past if we could. All of us would do some things (many things!) differently. However, we can all do something about today and tomorrow, beginning this very moment. Regardless of where you have been or what you have done, you can begin right now to do sex and marriage God's way. And remember this: God's way is always the best way in every way. That includes sex. That includes marriage.

As we prepare to look at the Song of Songs, God's instruction manual for sex and marriage, let's be reminded that good sex and a good marriage involve two important things: *commitment* and *hard work*. Why? Part of the answer is that men and women are so radically different, and they are different in so many ways. The Song of Songs will help us see many of these, and perhaps we will even have a little fun as we discover them. I recently came across a rather comical analysis that identifies a few of the differences that exist between men and women. There is nothing scientific about it, but it sure hits close to home. It also hints (rather loudly!) that if we will just slow down and pay a little attention, we can with a smile acknowledge and enjoy the differences that can add some "heavenly spice" to our marriages.

Ten Observations That Highlight the Difference
Between a Man and a Woman!

1. A man will pay $10 for a $5 item he wants.
    A woman will pay $5 for a $10 item that she doesn't want (or need).

2. A woman worries about the future until she gets a husband.
    A man never worries about the future until he gets a wife.

3. A successful man is one who makes more money than his wife can spend.
    A successful woman is one who can find such a man.

4. To be happy with a man you must understand him a lot and love him a little.

   To be happy with a woman you must love her a lot and not try to understand her at all.

5. Married men live longer than single men, but married men are a lot more willing to die.

6. Any married man should forget his mistakes; there's no reason for two people to remember the same things.

7. Men wake up as good-looking as they went to bed.

   Women somehow deteriorate during the night.

8. A woman marries a man expecting he will change, but he doesn't.

   A man marries a woman expecting that she won't change, but she does.

9. A woman has the last word in any argument. Anything a man says after that is the beginning of a new argument.

10. There are two times when a man doesn't understand a woman—before and after marriage.

One final word: A successful and lasting marriage will always be a triangle. It will involve a man, a woman, and God. Given the challenges of our day and the differences that exist between men and women, we dare not move forward without God taking the lead. God wants our marriages to succeed. He gave us a book to guide us. Let's see what He has to say.

Chapter 1

How to Begin a Love Story
THE SONG OF SONGS 1:1–8

What do love, romance, and marriage look like through the eyes of a child? I came across some answers that kids gave which might interest you.

> To the question, "How do you decide whom to marry?"
>
> Allen, age ten, said, "You've got to find someone who likes the same stuff. Like, if you like sports, she should like it, and she should keep the chips and dips coming."
>
> Kristin, age ten, replied, "No person really decides before they grow up who they're going to marry. God decides it all the way before, and you got to find out who you're stuck with."

> When asked, "How can a stranger tell if two people are married?"
>
> Derek, age eight, said, "Married people usually look happy to talk to other people."

A boy named Eddie responded, "You might have to guess based on whether they seem to be yelling at the same kids."

When asked, "Why do people go out on a date?"
Lynette, age eight, was rather straightforward from the female perspective: "Dates are for having fun, and people should use them to get to know each other. Even boys have something to say if you listen long enough."

And responding to the question, "How do you make a marriage work?"
A seven-year-old boy, wise beyond his years, said, "'Tell your wife that she looks pretty, even if she doesn't.'"

What do love, romance, and marriage look like through the eyes of a modern Washington writer and businessman? The opinion held by Philip Harvey is not nearly as hopeful or positive as that of the children surveyed above. In an article entitled "Divorce for the Best," Mr. Harvey said:

A reasonable level of divorce may be a symptom of a healthy and mobile society, a society in which men and women are living unprecendently long lives, lives for which the companionship of but a single other person for 30 or 40 or 50 years may simply be inappropriate. . . . That most Americans categorically oppose divorce on principle is a function more of our aspiration to the ideal state than a realistic acceptance of how we humans actually behave. . . .

The freedom to have more than one mate over a
75-year lifespan may be a positive thing. Is it not possible that the ideal companion for our younger child-
rearing years will not be the ideal companion for our
middle and later years? Is it not reasonable to suggest
that the radical differences in the way we live in our
fifties and sixties and beyond may be under many circumstances, most appropriately lived with a different
person from the one with whom we reared children? . . .
The interests of children must be given a very high priority. But allowing for that, it seems to me that a reasonable
level of divorce is more likely to be a quality of a mobile
and healthy modern society than a sign of moral decay.[1]

Harvey is not alone in his rather pessimistic prediction of one
man with one woman for life. James Dobson in his January 2000
newsletter shared that

Sandy Burchsted, an unmarried "futurist" from
Houston, estimates that one hundred years from now,
the average American will marry at least four times
and routinely engage in extramarital affairs with no
fear of public humiliation. Miss Burchsted, who is
writing a book on marriage in the year 2100, identified
what she believed will be four different types of marriage at a World Future Society conference in July,
1999. The first union is called the "*icebreaker
marriage*," (usually lasting about five years) in which
couples will learn how to live together and gain sexual
experience. Once disillusionment sets in, claims

Burchsted, it will be perfectly acceptable for the couple to divorce. If one of the partners decides to marry again, he or she will enter a *"parenting marriage,"* which lasts between 15 and 20 years. These couples will view raising children as their primary purpose, although child-rearing in the future will be in communal settings, not nuclear families.

After the second marriage is terminated, couples might enter a third union, which Burchsted calls the *"self-marriage."* This relationship will be focused on self-discovery and personal awareness. "We see marriage as a conscious, evolutionary process," says Burchsted, "so this marriage will be about consciously evolving yourself." Finally, there is a fourth category of marriage, which will emerge as a result of the theory that people in the twenty-first century will be living until at least the age of 120. Burchsted calls this late-in-life marriage the *"soul-mate connection,"* characterized by "marital bliss, shared spirituality, physical monogamy and equal partnership." *The Washington Times* says that Burchsted's theories are based on "trends showing women becoming more financially independent, marriage and childbearing becoming more 'delinked,' 'serial monogamy' becoming more acceptable and extramarital sexual affairs occurring more frequently and with less public outcry."[2]

Burchsted's views on our future sexual habits are shared by others as well. In an article in *Time* magazine the question was asked about the future of male-female relationships, "Will We Still Need to Have Sex?" Their answer: "Having sex is too much fun for us to stop, but religious convictions aside, it will be more for recreation than for procreation."[3] Another writer says, "Sex will be just for lust—babies will come from reproductive bank accounts."[4]

I am convinced God did not hardwire or program human persons to long for these kinds of shallow, pseudorelationships where any meaningful idea of love vanishes like an early morning mist vaporized by the sun. Let's go back to the Bible and see what the Creator says about how to begin a love story. I believe God is something of a cosmic romantic who enjoys a good love story. The Song of Songs, which is Solomon's, paints the portrait of such a love story and right from the start provides principles to get us off to a good start. How do you begin a love story?

Solomon's Finest Song
Oh that he would kiss me with the kisses of his mouth!
For your love is more delightful than wine.
The fragrance of your perfume is intoxicating;
your name is perfume poured out.
No wonder young women adore you.
Take me with you—let us hurry.
Oh that the king would bring me to his chambers.
We will rejoice and be glad for you;
we will praise your love more than wine.
It is only right that they adore you. (vv. 1–4)

ANTICIPATE THE REWARDS OF BEING WITH YOUR MATE (VV. 1–4)

This book is entitled "The Song of Songs, Which is Solomon's" or "Solomon's Finest Song." First Kings 4:32 indicates

Solomon authored 1,005 songs, but out of all of them this is his "finest song"; this is his best. The second-century rabbi Akiba ben Joseph said of the Song of Songs, "In the entire world there is nothing to equal the day in which the Song of Songs was given to Israel. All the writings are holy, but the Song of Songs is the holy of holies" (Mishnah, Yadaim 3:5).[5] In other words, this was the number one song of the Jerusalem hit parade in 1000 B.C.! First Kings 4:29–31 also teaches us that God blessed Solomon with wisdom that exceded all his contemporaries. Here Solomon looks at the issue of marriage and romance. Marriage is God's good gift. It should be a blessing. It should be rewarding. What kind of rewards does Solomon outline for us?

DESIRE THE PHYSICAL PLEASURES OF MARRIAGE (VV. 1–2)

Marriage is the context in which physical passion and pleasure is set free. The kiss is a universal expression of desire and affection, and the woman (she is called Shulammite in 6:13) expresses her desire for her lover to kiss her and to kiss her deeply and repeatedly. The senses of touch and taste come together, and the resulting passion is more than she can handle. She says, "Your love is more delightful than wine." By describing his romantic, affectionate kisses in this way, she is saying, "I find the touch of your lips and the embrace of your mouth sweet, powerful, intoxicating. It sweeps me off my feet. It sets my head to spinning." The passionate kiss, we have discovered, is a telltale sign of a healthy, romantic marriage, even more than sex. "The passionate kiss (avg. length one minute) reveals a lot about your relationship. Considered even more intimate than sex, passionate smooching is one of the first things to go when spouses aren't getting along."[6] Several years ago I heard of a survey taken in Germany that revealed that if a man kissed his wife in the morning before leaving for work, he would: (1) live five years longer, (2) have 50 percent fewer illnesses, and (3) make 20 to 30 percent more money than one who doesn't! Proverbs 5:18–19 says, "Take pleasure in the wife of your youth. A loving doe, a graceful fawn—let her breasts always satisfy you; be lost in her love forever."

EXPERIENCE THE PERSONAL PLEASURES OF MARRIAGE (VV. 3–4)

The word *love* occurs repeatedly in verses 2–7. A careful examination reveals love's connection to the mind, will, and emotions. Not only does love connect our intellects and our desires, but it also keeps them in proper balance. Love is to be a delightful experience that expresses itself in many ways. Love has a physical dimension, but it is not just physical. The Song gives us four avenues whereby lovers should enjoy each other.

Delight in their fragrance (v. 3a). The thought of the physical caresses of romance calls to mind not only the intoxication of wine but also the sweet smell of his cologne. He tastes good, and he smells good. Without stretching the text, he brushed his teeth and used mouthwash. He took a bath, used soap, and then anointed himself with "good ointments." This is good counsel for every man at any time! Already we see the senses of taste, touch, and smell come together in the pursuit of romance and love. Here is a man sensitive to the things his woman finds attractive. She is appreciative and responds in kind.

Delight in their fame (v. 3b). His kisses are intoxicating. His smell is exhilarating. His reputation is unquestioned. "Your name [meaning his reputation and character] is perfume poured out." A person is more than their physical appearance. Who one really is goes beneath the skin. Wise people, when dating, will not only form an opinion of the person with whom they are involved; they will also listen and hear what others have to say.

No matter how strong the physical attraction, they will also listen to public opinion. Is he honest? Trustworthy? Does she possess a calm spirit? A level head? Is he known as a playboy? Does she have friends who believe in her? We should carefully consider what others say about the person we date, the person we would consider marrying. We all have blind spots. Love can indeed be blind. We must not let our emotions override good decision making, even if it hurts. Shulammite knew this man was respected. He was known as a person of character and integrity. She was not only physically attracted to him; she could respect him. She could admire him.

Delight in their friends (vv. 3c, 4b). Solomon was a much-desired man. He was indeed a catch! Verse 3 says, "No wonder young women adore you." In verse 4 these same women exclaim, concerning Shulammite's good fortune, "We will rejoice and be glad for you; we will praise your love more than wine." The esteem of other women enhances Shulammite's love and admiration for the man in her life. In essence they are saying, "If you don't get him and keep him, then we are going after him." Any woman would be fortunate to have such a man as her own.

Delight in their faithfulness (v. 4a). While it is the case that potential rivals are lurking about, this woman is so secure in her relationship with her man that she can allow and rejoice in the praise and admiration showered on him by others. Love, to be sure, is jealous (cf. 8:6), yet it can also be generous when the bond is secure. She knows at the right time she can ask him to "take me with you—let us hurry" (v. 4) and he will. He is her king, and she is his queen. Their love is majestic and royal. On one plane she can share him publicly and with others. On another level she possesses him as her own, and there are things that only the two of them share, and that, in private. He brings her, and only her, into his chambers. This is an exclusive love that dare not be shared with another.[7]

In a survey *Glamour* magazine asked men which marriage vow was the hardest to keep: 19 percent said it was to love "in sickness and in health"; 19 percent said it was to love "for richer or for poorer." The toughest of all, said 60 percent of the men, was "to forsake all others."[8] A woman should be confident in her man's faithfulness. Ephesians 5:33 says it well, "Each one of you [husbands] is to love his wife as himself."

> *O daughters of Jerusalem,*
>> *I am dark like the tents of Kedar,*
>> *yet lovely like the curtains of Solomon.*
> *Do not stare at me because I am dark,*
>> *for the sun has gazed on me.*
> *My mother's sons were angry with me;*
>> *they made me a keeper of the vineyards.*
>> *My own vineyard I have not kept.*
> *Tell me, you whom I love:*
>> *Where do you pasture your sheep?*
>> *Where do you let them rest at noon?*
> *Why should I be like one who veils herself*
>> *beside the flocks of your companions? (vv. 1:5–7)*

Accept the Realities of Being with Your Mate (vv. 5–7)

Marriage has its romance, its rewards. It also has its rough spots and realities. Men anticipating marriage may think, *Wow!*

We'll spend all of our time in the bed. Well, I've got some news for you. Hopefully you will enjoy some marvelous time in the bed and in other places. You will, however, spend the majority of your time out of bed, and you will need to face head-on some of the realities that will confront you as you try to build your marriage. Let's note two realities a man must face when living with a woman. This list, by the way, is by no means exhaustive. It's just a place to start!

A WOMAN CAN BE AMBIVALENT CONCERNING HER APPEARANCE (VV. 5–6)

Women change. It is their prerogative as females. It is built into their genes. They change, and they can change quickly and often. A man must be alert and sensitive. Like a weather radar, he must be able to see what is on the horizon.

How a woman thinks she looks is extremely important to her. It goes to the foundation of her self-worth. In particular, she wants to know that she is attractive to the man in her life. But guys, we must understand, what she thinks about how she looks matters more to her than what we think about how she looks.

She may be delighted with her appearance (vv. 5–6). Shulammite knew she possessed a natural beauty. She believed that she was pretty and attractive, lovely and pleasing in appearance. She was sensitive to the fact that men are creatures of sight and that they are moved by what they see. She was confident he would like what he saw when he looked at her. Of herself she can say, "I am . . . lovely."

She may be defensive with her appearance (v. 6a). A tan was not grand in Solomon's day. Women prized fair skin and the "indoor look." This would signify the lofty social standing of the well-to-do city girl. In contrast Shulammite was deeply suntanned and dark. She was a country girl who had been "looked upon" negatively by both the sun of nature and the sons of her mother who forced her to labor in the vineyards. "She had been doubly burned, by the sun, and by her brother's anger."[9] "The tents of Kedar" speaks of "the Bedouin tribes whose tents, made from the hair of the black goats so common among them, are a frequent sight on the fringes of the deserts."[10] "The curtains of Solomon" draw a different analogy. These curtains would be beautiful and valuable, of "exquisite craftsmanship. . . . She is both hardened by the elements and yet beautiful."[11]

She may be disappointed with her appearance (v. 6b). She worked hard to tend the vineyards in the field. As a result, her own vineyard, her body, had been neglected. Unable to give the time, attention, and care she would have liked, her physical appearance, at least to her way of thinking, was less than the best. One easily senses her pain, her insecurity. Tom Gedhill writes:

> Her vineyard represents everything that conveys her
> essential femininity. Her looks, her complexion, her
> dress, her status, her sexuality—all those considera-
> tions which would make her attractive to a man. . . . In
> these verses we are brought face to face with the prob-
> lems of our own self-image. How do we view our-
> selves? When we look at our own reflection in the mir-
> ror, do we like what we see? Can we accept ourselves as
> we really are, with all our quirks, idiosyncrasies and
> limitations? Do we like the way we look? Or are we
> always wishing we were like someone else?[12]

A woman's appearance is an important area in her life. It requires on the part of a man great sensitivity and understanding.

Men, make sure you praise her and build her up. Don't be like the husband whose wife walked out of the closet one day wearing a new dress and asked, "Honey, does this dress make me look fat?" To which he responded, "Nah, your hips make you look fat." Such a response will do neither your wife nor you any good.

A WOMAN CAN BE ANXIOUS CONCERNING HIS ABSENCE (V. 7)

Security is important to a marriage. A man feels it when his mate praises him. A woman feels it when her man is present. A marriage is destined to suffer and suffer greatly if there are extended periods of unhealthy separation.

A husband's absence can be a source of personal sorrow (v. 7a). Solomon is gone. Why we are not told, though the imagery implies he is about the normal duties of life. Here the picture is of a shepherd tending his sheep. She misses him. She longs for him. To speak so frankly exposes her heart, but it would also excite the heart of her lover. At noon the sheep would sleep. The other shepherds would be resting. There would be time just for them. No distractions. No interruptions. She wants him at any cost. Furthermore, what a creative lady we see. Their meeting would be outside in the wide open spaces, perhaps under a shade tree? Perhaps in a temporary hut or shelter? Even as she sorrows over his absence, she strategizes about how to make their intimate time together new, exciting, and memorable. But you can't love them if you're not with them.

A husband's absence can be a source of personal shame (v. 7b). To wear a veil as she wandered among the other flocks and shepherds would be embarrassing. It could, in that day, give the impression that she was a prostitute or possibly in mourning. A prostitute has many men, but she has no man she can call her own. There is no one at whom she can point and say, that man is my man and this woman is his woman. She did not want there to be the slightest doubt that he was hers and she was his. For there to be even a question of their fidelity and commitment to each other would be shameful. Shulammite knew there was a cost, a price to be paid, in committing herself for a lifetime to another person. She was aware of the fact that a marriage relationship can sometimes become high profile and take on a fishbowl type of scrutiny. Still, she was willing to accept and live up to such a challenge. Each of us must be willing to do the same.

> *If you don't know for yourself,*
>   *most beautiful of women,*
>   *follow the tracks of the flock,*
> *and pasture your young goats*
>   *near the shepherds' tents. (v. 8)*

ACKNOWLEDGE THE RISK OF BEING WITH YOUR MATE (V. 8)

This romance thing is risky business. You take a chance. You roll the dice. There are, however, ways to improve the odds in your favor. Verse 8 is best understood as a mild, maybe even a playful, rebuke of Shulammite. She is looking to "hook up" with her man. What does she need to do?

KNOW WHERE YOU CAN FIND HIM

Shulammite is called "most beautiful of women," yet she is teased for not knowing where her man is. Perhaps she doesn't, as of yet, know him as well as she should. After all, marriage is a lifelong learning process. It is imperative that we grow in knowledge of our mate, of our mate's needs, disposition, gifts, weaknesses, and inclinations. To love our mates we must know them and know where and how to find them when we want them.

GO WHERE YOU CAN FIND THEM

Knowledge must be accompanied by action. How often is it in a relationship that we know the right thing to do but we do not do the right thing? Shulammite is told to follow what, in essence, are familiar paths or "tracks" which Solomon is known to walk. If she will follow the familiar paths, she will find him. The rest we leave to a sanctified imagination.

Researchers Howard Markman and Scott Stanley of the University of Denver help us understand, in part, why good marriages work and bad marriages fail. It's not sex, money, or how many fights you have that make for a happy union. Marriage-wise couples aren't afraid to accept influence from each other. They connect on a daily basis in many small ways, think about their partner periodically when they're apart, take time-outs to soothe tempers, use humor as a coolant in arguments, and have softer start-ups when fighting. Even in conflict, their ratio of positive to negative actions—from a simple "mmmmh" or "yeah" to a pat on the arm—are 5 to 1 as opposed to 0.8 to 1 for unstable marriages.[13]

This is sound advice. We should be influenced by each other. The Lord should influence us. We should learn from each other. We should learn from God. We must grow in our knowledge of each other. Let me conclude with some sound advice that will help move us in the right direction as we think about marriage and as we think about each other.

GETTING STARTED ON THINKING ABOUT MARRIAGE

If we would raise our marriages to the level God intends, we must guide them with principles that focus more on *we* than *me* and that esteem the other better than self. What we are after is having the mind of Christ (Phil. 2:2–5).

Here are seven areas that need our careful *thinking* and *commitment.*

1. Educationally

- Study marriage; become a real student of it.
- Study the opposite sex; at least *try* to become an expert on them. (Be ready for a lifetime adventure!)
- Study *your* spouse; really get to know her/him.

2. Sexually

- Be faithful to each other for life. Put boundaries in place now and commit never to compromise them.
- Know the difference between your needs and your wants.
- Exercise self-control; resist outside temptations.
- Never bargain with sex. Don't become a marital prostitute. (To play you must pay!) This is a lose-lose proposition.
- Make sure there is mutual consent to all you and your spouse decide to do (1 Cor. 7:1–7). If a spouse cannot say no when circumstances warrant it, how can that spouse be sure that she or he is not a slave?
- Do not expect your spouse to have the same appetites and desires that you have. Strive for compatible appetites.

3. Individually

- Do not make unilateral decisions that affect your relationship.

- Do not depend primarily on your spouse for a sense of self-worth. Look to God.
- Own up to your own mistakes. Be willing to say seven magical words, "I am sorry, will you forgive me?" (Eph. 4:32).
- Deal with your own sins first before dealing with your mate's (Gal. 6:1).

4. Publicly

- Keep confidential matters confidential.
- Never criticize your spouse in public or in front of others.
- Guard the way you dress; check your motives and your judgment.

5. Parentally

- Set up disciplinary policies jointly and stick to them (Eph. 6:1–4).
- Do not argue about discipline in front of the children.
- Be loving and always restore fellowship after discipline.
- Discipline in a manner that is appropriate to the child's action, age, and maturity.

6. Financially

- Set up financial priorities jointly and stick to them.
- Remember, no one is entitled to a superior status just because one earns the money to pay the rent and buy the groceries. Keeping the house clean and guiding the home front efficiently is just as important and just as worthy of appreciation and praise.
- All who share in the labor to maintain the family ought to share in everything the family earns or produces.

7. Relationally

- Take each other seriously but not too seriously.
- Nurture each other (Eph. 5:29–30).

- Set up a problem-solving strategy.
- Be respectful and courteous at all times. Treat your mate like a good friend.
- Spend time with your spouse and family (both quality and quantity).
- Make room for intimacy and affection without pushing for sex. (Guys, are you paying attention?)
- Treat each other as equals because you are.
- Be honest with each other; always speak the truth in love (Eph. 4:15).
- Give your spouse practical and relational priority in all aspects of your life.
- Be slow to anger, slow to speak, and quick to listen (James 1:19).
- Do not let the sun go down on your anger (Eph. 4:29).
- Never stop caring about pleasing your spouse (Phil. 2:3–4).
- Seek unity and do not feel threatened by disagreement (Phil. 2:2).
- Honor each other's rights and needs.
- Do not impose your will on the other. Be peaceful and kind and use persuasion, not coercion.
- Seek to be each other's best friend.
- Try to deal with facts rather than feelings.
- Minister to rather than manipulate each other.
- Put your spouse before all others including the children.
- Honor the Creator's structure for marriage (Eph. 5:21–33).
- Be approachable, teachable, and correctable (even by, and especially by, your spouse).
- Do not try to control everything.

- Confront each other with tenderness, compassion, and loving concern, and take pains not to exasperate your spouse.
- Be willing to sacrifice for your loved ones.
- Do not neglect your responsibility to provide for your own.
- Be willing to communicate and to listen.
- Despise divorce and determine it will never be an option.
- Eat as many meals with one another as possible.
- Whenever possible, postpone doing things you want to do for yourself to the times when your spouse is busy with other things.
- Do not stop trying to make time for your spouse just because it seems so impossible to do so.

Chapter 2

The Power of Praising Your Partner

THE SONG OF SONGS 1:9–14

In their outstanding book *The Gift of the Blessing,* Gary Smalley and John Trent give us some biblical and practical tips on how we can *bless* rather than *curse* those we love. When it comes to marriage and our mate, their counsel is crucial and invaluable. They write:

> God has put us together in such a way that we have emotional and physical needs that can only be met by affirmation, acceptance as to intrinsic worth, encouragement, and unconditional love. We all have the desire and need to receive "the blessing" from others. Others include our heavenly Father but it should also include our spouse. Neither is to be excluded if we are to receive true holistic blessings.
>
> The essential elements of the blessings include five things:
>
> 1. **A meaningful touch**—This includes hand-holding, hugging, kissing, and all types of

25

bodily contact that have the purpose of communicating love and affection.

2. **A spoken word**—This element can demonstrate love and a sense of worth by the time
involved, and the message(s) delivered. Its
repetitive nature is crucial.

3. **Expression of high value**—This involves our
passing along a message to others that affirms
their intrinsic worth and value as a person.
Praising them as valuable is the key idea.

4. **Picturing a special future**—This is the
uniquely prophetic aspect of the blessing.
What do our words tell others we believe the
future holds for them? How do our present
descriptions (nicknames) of others lay the
foundation for future attitudes and actions on
their part? How often it is that children fulfill
the earlier expectations and predictions of a
parent and friends, for good or bad. Positive
words of encouragement as to future possibili-
ties are those that will bless rather than curse.

5. **An active commitment to see the blessing
come to pass**—This characteristic is both
God-ward and man-ward. Godwardly, we
are to commit others to His blessing and
will. Manwardly, we are personally to make
the commitment to spend whatever time,
energy and resources necessary to bless
others.[1]

When I examine Gary and John's list, I discover that blessing others involves both what I say and what I do. Words are important. Actions matter. Further, what I say and do cannot be occasional. They must be constant. They also must be specific, sacrificial, and even sensual. Now you might ask, where did you get these ideas, especially the last one? The answer is found in Song of Songs 1:9–14 where Solomon tells us, "There is power in praising your partner." Here we see important and essential aspects of how to praise, how to bless our partner.

> *I compare you, my darling,*
> > *to a mare among Pharaoh's chariots.*
> *Your cheeks are beautiful with jewelry—*
> > *your neck with its necklace. (vv. 9–10)*

BE SPECIFIC IN YOUR PRAISE (VV. 9–10)

Verse 9 shifts the scene from the simple world of the shepherd to the splendid world of the Egyptian Pharaoh. Solomon is aware of Shulammite's ambivalence and insecurity about her appearance and his absence (vv. 5–8). His spousal antenna is active, and it is picking up signals. She needs him to bless her, to affirm her, to tell her she's the best. That is exactly what he does.

TELL HER SHE IS SPECIAL (V. 9)

Solomon begins by calling her "my darling" (the NKJV has "my love"). This is the first but not the last time Solomon will address her in this way (cf. 1:15, 2:2, 10, 13; 4:1, 7; 5:2; 6:4). Repeatedly (nine times!) Solomon tells her of his love. Unlike her brothers who hurt her in verse 6, Solomon will treat her with TLC.

He will be her provider and protector, her lover and friend. She is his love.

Solomon then does something that, if a man in America were to do this in our day, he would probably find himself in a hole from which he would never extricate himself. He compares his lover to a horse! Specifically, he says you are like "a mare among Pharaoh's chariots." We are stunned by such a statement. She, however, would have been greatly honored. Pharaoh's chariots were pulled by stallions. A mare among them would have caused quite a commotion. She is likened to an only female in a world of males! What incredible value. She is, in his estimation, utterly priceless. She is desired not just by him but also by others. Yet he is the fortunate one who has captured her heart. She is unique; she is special.

TELL HER SHE IS BEAUTIFUL (V. 10)

Solomon now focuses on one of the areas of her insecurity: her looks. Her "cheeks" are lovely, beautiful. They are enhanced with the dangling earrings, the ornaments and jewelry that grace them. Her "neck" is also beautiful "with its necklace." She is regal and impressive. A stately dignity emanates from her person. The bridles of chariot horses were often decorated in beautiful and elaborate jewelry and Solomon may still have the image of the lovely mare in mind. However, by now it is in the back of his mind as he gazes upon the beauty of his love. Her adornments do not detract but enhance her appearance. Solomon is not looking at some "overdressed glittering Christmas tree."[2] There is nothing extravagant or excessive about her. A simple beauty is perhaps the best beauty. In Solomon's opinion she has no equal, and he tells her so.

Words are powerful weapons. "Sticks and stones may break my bones but names or words can never hurt me" is not true.

I have a scar over my eye where my cousin hit me in the eye with a baseball bat when I was a small boy. I have another scar on my right ear where my brother body-slammed me on a marble coffee table one day when we were wrestling. Mom, of course, was gone somewhere, thank goodness. I have yet another scar right under my chin where a friend (I think!) rammed his football helmet while we played "bull-in-the-ring" before a big game one Friday night. Now let me tell you, all three of those events inflicted serious pain on my person. They hurt! However, none of the three wounded me as badly as have some words that have been fired at me at different times in my life.

Steve Stephens reminds us, "A healthy marriage is a safe haven from the tensions of everyday life. We need to hear positive things from our mate." He then lists thirty-seven things we should say to our spouse. Any spouse will be blessed by the following:

"Good job!"

"You are wonderful."

"That was really great."

"You look gorgeous today."

"I don't feel complete without you."

"I appreciate all the things you've done for me all these years."

"You come first in my life, before kids, career, friends, anything."

"I'm glad I married you."

"You're the best friend I have."

"If I had to do it over again, I'd still marry you."

"I wanted you today."

"I missed you today."

"I couldn't get you out of my mind today."

"It's nice to wake up next to you."

"I will always love you."

"I love to see your eyes sparkle when you smile."

"As always, you look good today."

"I trust you."

"I can always count on you."

"You make me feel good."

"I'm so proud to be married to you."

"I'm sorry."

"I was wrong."

"What would you like?"

"What is on your mind?"

"Let me just listen."

"You are so special."

"I can't imagine life without you."

"I wish I were a better partner."

"What can I do to help?"

"Pray for me."

"I'm praying for you today."

"I prize every moment we spend together."

"Thank you for loving me."

"Thank you for accepting me."

"Thank you for being my partner."

"You make every day brighter."[3]

Be particular in your praise. It will speak to your mate's heart and create an environment of romance, which is essential for building the intimate aspects of a relationship.

We will make gold jewelry for you,
accented with silver. (v. 11)

BE SACRIFICIAL IN YOUR PRAISE (V. 11)

Solomon's praise of Shulammite inspires the praise of others. What we publicly say about our mate will often influence the opinion of others about them. Solomon has told her she is special and beautiful. She is the best. She deserves the best, but not just in words, also in actions. When a man wants to be a blessing to his wife, here are two things he should always remember:

BE SPECIFIC

"Gold jewelry, accented with silver" is now presented to Shulammite. Gedhill, in his free paraphrase says, "We'll crown you with more royalty, O maiden queen, with costly gems, with rings of golden sheen and sparkling spikes of silver."[4] Socrates said, "By all means marry. If you get a good wife, you'll become happy. If you get a bad one, you'll become a philosopher." I am convinced that the issue is not so much a man "getting" a good wife as it is a man "gaining" a good wife by the way he loves her, by the way he cares for her. Women love specific and creative ideas. A man who invites his wife out on a date only to tell her it doesn't matter where we go or what we do doesn't know women. Love is specific. Praise is specific. Judy Bodner in her book *When Love Dies: How to Save a Hopeless Marriage* drops a few hints to help husbands: (1) leave notes and love letters around; (2) plan detailed getaways; (3) set aside time alone just for the two of you; (4) share your feelings with each other; (5) make sexual intimacy attractive by creating a bedroom that is inviting and pleasant, a place of beauty.

BE SINCERE

The gifts of Solomon are genuine and from the heart. He is not trying to bribe her or buy her. His desire is to bless her and to do so in a way that speaks to her heart. Solomon had learned, or was at least in the process of learning, to speak her "love language." Gary Chapman, in his wonderful book *The Five Love Languages,* points out that every person speaks at least one of five love languages. Some are even equipped to speak several, and with varying dialects. However, it is rare that a husband and wife speak the same love language. After all, opposites do attract. Gary identifies the five love languages as:

1. Words of Affirmation
2. Receiving Gifts
3. Acts of Service
4. Quality Time
5. Physical Touch

In our marriage it is clear that Charlotte and I have two love languages each. Not surprising, they are distinctively different. Hers are receiving gifts and quality time. Mine are words of affirmation and physical touch. I always strike a chord in Charlotte's heart if I bring her a gift. Cost is never a factor; it truly is the thought that counts. When I block off time for the two of us, she also responds in a positive and receptive manner.

I've often wondered if her love languages are somehow related to her childhood and teenage years. Charlotte's parents were alcoholics, and they divorced when she was a little girl. She has told me that she had some pretty unspectacular birthdays and Christmases. At about the age of nine, she and her brother and sister were placed in a children's home, where she spent the next ten years of her life. She really never saw either her mom or dad during those years except for a couple of times early on. Time spent with family and receiving gifts from them just didn't happen. I'm certain this may have, at least in some measure, shaped her two love languages.

Let me add before I move on that one wonderful thing did happen to Charlotte while she was in the children's home. She received Jesus Christ as her personal Lord and Savior, and God became her perfect heavenly Father. Since then He has been molding and shaping her into the beautiful godly woman, wife, and mother she is today.

My love languages are altogether different from hers. I love it when she praises me, when she affirms me with her words. It means the world to me. I also love her touch and in lots of ways and places! One in particular is especially needful—my feet. I love to have my feet rubbed. When I get to heaven, I have already put in a request for two angels: one to rub and massage the left foot and one to rub and massage the right foot.

I remember one evening Charlotte asked me to watch a movie with her (her love language of time) called *Sense and Sensibility*. It was immediately clear to me that this would not be an action-packed thriller. I quickly began to offer my best excuses as to why I just couldn't "waste," I mean give up, that much time. To my amazement she didn't argue with me. As she said OK and walked away, she casually said, "I understand. I'm sorry you will miss out on the two-hour foot massage that accompanies the popcorn and the movie." I had only one response to that, "What time does the movie start?" A couple that grows in their knowledge of one another will learn to speak the love language of their mate. They will do it specifically, and they will do it sincerely.

While the king is on his couch,
  my perfume releases its fragrance.
My love is a sachet of myrrh to me,
  spending the night between my breasts.
My love is a cluster of henna blossoms to me,
  in the vineyards of En-gedi. (vv. 12–14)

BE SENSUAL IN YOUR PRAISE (VV. 12–14)

Shulammite is moved to respond to the loving overtures of Solomon. Her insecurities have vanished. Her anxieties have been put to rest by his words and actions of love. She now returns the favor. What we see is the two of them trying to outdo the other in the game of love. This will continue for several verses. What a wonderful contest for a couple to engage in. Let the games begin! Shulammite has strong desires for her man. They are personal, physical, and sensual. They are particular and passionate. How do we, with intentionality, make our desires, our feelings, known to our mate?

DESIRE IS MADE KNOWN BY LOVE (V. 12)

(Tell him he is *worthy* of an expensive display.)

Again the man is addressed as a "king," as royalty. Reclining "on his couch" or "at his table" indicates a time of rest and relaxation. Men have as a basic need for "home support and serenity." (We will address this later.) Shulammite knows what her man needs, and she provides it. Her perfume, nard, was expensive and "derived from a plant native to the Himalayan region of India. The scarcity, and hence the value, of this exotic fragrance made it much in demand as a 'love-potion.'"[5] Appealing to his self-worth and sense of smell, Shulammite, who is aroused herself, seeks to elicit the same from her man. He is her king and worthy of a sensual and expensive display of affection. One can only imagine his response.

DESIRE IS MADE KNOWN BY LOYALTY (V. 13)

(Tell him he is a fragrance close to your heart.)

In genuinely erotic tones the woman says, "My love is a sachet of myrrh to me spending the night between my breasts."

> Myrrh is a resinous gum gathered from a species of a
> South Arabian tree. . . . In liquid form it would be carried in small bottles like nard, but it was also used in
> solid form. This way it could be carried in a small cloth
> pouch or sachet and worn next to the body. . . . The
> myrrh was mixed with fat . . . as the fat melted from
> the body heat, the aroma of the myrrh . . . would fill
> the room.[6]

Shulammite compares Solomon to this precious, sweet-smelling bundle that lies all night between her breasts, close to her heart. "Her thoughts of him are as fragrant and refreshing as the perfume that rises before her. . . . She carries those fragrant thoughts of him through the night in peaceful sleep."[7] Nestled between her breasts against her beating heart, there is an intimate bond of love, longing, and loyalty that cannot be broken. There is a connection, a commitment that virtually transcends words. In an article entitled "The Danger of Divorce," Norman Bales says, "Perhaps the strongest deterrent to divorce is commitment. Every marriage will be tested at some point. What's the difference between those who survive the test and those who don't? Commitment tops the list."[8] There was a commitment, a loyalty between Shulammite and Solomon. All night he lay as a precious perfume between her breasts, close to her heart.

DESIRE IS MADE KNOWN BY LONGING (V. 14)

(Tell him he is refreshing like an oasis in a desert.)

Again Shulammite refers to Solomon as "my love." Theirs is an exclusive love relationship. He is a one-woman kind of man, and she is a one-man kind of woman. But she says more. He is refreshing, like "a cluster of henna blossoms to me, in the vineyards of En-gedi." The henna bush can reach a height of ten feet. It has thick yellow and white flowers in clusters and smells like roses. A semitropical vegetation, it grows at the En-gedi Oasis on the western shore of the Dead Sea, south of Jerusalem. The flowers are beautiful to see and sweet to smell, and a rare find in a desert's arid climate.

The analogy is striking. Solomon is like an oasis with its surprising pleasures and provisions in a desert. He is a rare find and therefore of inestimable value. It is as if the woman is saying, "All I have seen is a desert of men until I met you. You are my oasis with your beauty and fragrance. No man refreshed me until I met you. I dream about you; I think about you. I dream about us. I think about us." Unbelievable, is it not, the passion that flows from a little praise. *Passion in the bedroom is preceded by passion in all the other rooms.* There is power in praising your partner.

Tommy Nelson well says, "Kindness is a mark of respect. Respect is necessary for romance."[9] We have seen a couple who deeply and genuinely respected each other. We have seen a couple sensitive to the needs of the other. We have seen a couple determined to bless the other. We have seen a couple learning to speak each other's love language. What we have seen is wonderful. What we have seen can be our experience as well when we do romance God's way.

Chapter 3

How to Fan the Flames of Love

THE SONG OF SONGS 1:15–2:7

Romance and marriage, at least in any traditional sense, has fallen on hard times. This is especially true with younger Americans whose theme appears to be "sex without strings and relationships without rings." Now it must be acknowledged that the idea of "free love" is not a recent phenomenon. We can thank the 1960s and 1970s for that. Still, today's younger generation is clearly more interested in economic security and sexual self-gratification. At least that's the word out of Rutgers University and the National Marriage Project.

Today's young adults think living together as a trial run for marriage, or as an alternative to marriage, is the way to go. Sex is for fun, divorce is to be feared, and marriage is risky business and a potential economic hazard.

Yet, there is a surprising twist to all of this. In spite of their hesitancy and skepticism toward marriage, most young Americans still anticipate meeting their "soul mate" who will love them and meet their needs. The problem, however, is their "mercenary dating habits" are not likely to help them find their soul mate. Self-centeredness is not a formula for being the right mate, much less finding the right mate. And as one ages, the prospect pool has a nasty habit of growing smaller. This is a tragic reality, especially for women.[1]

What a tragic, but realistic picture of the mating and marriage scene today! However, Iris Krasnow of the *Washington Post* (Sept. 11, 2000) helps put all of this in perspective with her commentary on the HBO blockbuster "Sex and the City." In an article entitled "Being Single, Seeing Double" she writes:

> I'm looking at the recent *Time* magazine cover that pictures the four buffed stars of HBO's "Sex and the City," women who talk dirtier and have more sex than anyone I have ever met. Front and center is Sarah Jessica Parker, with her tumbles of long locks, perfectly highlighted and curled, falling to breasts encased in a white strapless gown. Her lips are glossed into an iridescent purple pout; the look in her cat-green eyes says, "Take me now."
>
> Decked for an evening of prowling, these women appear to be appropriate cover art for an article titled "How to Snag a Mate." Instead the "Sex and the City" sirens are a tease for a story on "Who Needs a Husband?," which points to a growing trend defined this way: "More women are saying no to marriage and embracing the single life. Are They Happy? . . ."
>
> Happy is not among the first words that come to mind. They are clearly stunning on the outside, but they do not exude real joy from within, and any single woman who has been dating too long and too much

can tell you why: Sex in the city feels good for fleeting
moments; it's no ticket to a satisfaction that endures.
And there lies the ancient reason why most Americans
still choose to get married. Being single is lonely.
Humans need long-term companionship.

Most women don't want intimacy on the fly with a
carousel of lovers. Most women want to finally find a
partner who looks beyond the bottle-gold fibers of
highlighted hair, and into the fiber of their being. Most
women want to be able to skip shaving their legs once
in a while and still feel beautiful in the eyes of their
men.

Bottom line: men and women have not changed deep down
inside where it really counts. All of us, no one is excluded, are
looking for love, and a love that will last. However, once we do find
it, how do we keep it, and keep it for a lifetime? Solomon would
say, "by fanning the flames." James Russell Lowell in his poem
entitled "Love" wrote:

True love is,
A love that shall be new and fresh *each hour,*
As is the sunset's golden mystery
Or the sweet coming of the evening star,
Alike, and yet most unlike, *every day,*
And seeming ever best and fairest *now.*

I like that. It speaks to my heart and my soul. It sounds like
the kind of love that lasts. God's Word is interested in a love that
lasts, a love that daily needs the flames of its fire stoked to a

passionate burning. How is such a love achieved? In The Song of Songs 1:15–2:7 we discover three helpful suggestions: (1) praise your partner, (2) proclaim their provision, and (3) prepare for passion.

> *How beautiful you are, my darling*
> > *How very beautiful!*
> > *Your eyes are doves.*

> *How handsome you are, my love.*
> > *How delightful!*
> > *Our bed is lush with foliage;*
> *the beams of our house are cedars,*
> > *and our rafters are cypresses.*
> *I am a rose of Sharon,*
> *a lily of the valleys.*

> *Like a lily among thorns,*
> > *so is my darling among the young women. (1:15–2:2)*

PRAISE YOUR PARTNER (1:15–2:2)

Praising our partner is a constant theme in the Song of Songs because it is an essential ingredient for a healthy marriage. Again and again we see the man praising his lady and the lady praising her man. Communication that consists of gracious and kind words is the currency that buys and builds a lasting love relationship. Previously, we noted the blessings that flow when we say positive things to and about our mate. It might be uncomfortable, but it is probably helpful if we also examine some things we should not say. Our friend Steve Stephens (whose "37 Things You Should Say to Your Spouse" were cited earlier) is again a big help when he writes:

> There is nothing more painful than having unhealthy communication with the one you love. It is through communication that we connect and our spirits touch. If that connection becomes contaminated, it is only a matter of time before the whole relationship is poisoned. In the process of communication, wisdom is [sometimes] knowing what not to say rather than what to say. . . .
>
> Therefore, I gathered together some close friends and asked them what not to say to your spouse. Here is their list:
>
> "I told you so."
> "You're just like your mother."
> "You're always in a bad mood."
> "You just don't think."
> "It's your fault."
> "What's wrong with you?"
> "All you ever do is complain."
> "I can't do anything to please you."
> "You get what you deserve."
> "Why don't you ever listen to me?"
> "Can't you be more responsible?"
> "What were you thinking?"
> "You're impossible!"

"I don't know why I put up with you."
"I can talk to you until I'm blue in the face and it
    doesn't do any good."
"I can do whatever I like."
"If you don't like it, you can just leave."
"Can't you do anything right?"
"That was stupid."
"All you ever do is think of yourself."
"If you really loved me, you'd do this."
"You're such a baby."
"Turnabout's fair play."
"You deserve a dose of your own medicine."
"What's your problem?"
"I can never understand you."
"Do you always have to be right?"[2]

Both Solomon and Shulammite knew the importance of words. Both were interested in fanning the flames of love. They continue their contest to see who can outpraise and outcompliment the other. What are the particulars of their praise with which they challenge us?

ADMIRE THEIR ATTRACTIVENESS (VV. 15–16)

Solomon tells his bride "how beautiful you are, my darling." "My darling" can also be translated "my love." This is not the first time Solomon has complimented her appearance. Perhaps once is not enough. I asked Charlotte one time if I could ever tell her too often, "I love you," and, "I think you are beautiful." Her answer was "absolutely not!" She said she never got tired of my praising her or of my saying, "I love you."

Solomon also says to Shulammite, "Your eyes are doves." "Beautiful eyes were a hallmark of perfection in a woman (cf. Rachel and Leah, Gen. 29:17). Rabbinic tradition identifies beautiful eyes with a beautiful personality."[3] Solomon, as he looked into her eyes, saw gentleness and tranquility, purity and simplicity. Her eyes were an eloquent witness to the radiant woman on the inside. Our eyes are a significant communication device. Outside of our words they are our most important and effective means of communication.

When we lived in Dallas, Texas, there was a woman who attended our church who was one mean lady. I have often said, somewhat playfully, that on any night there was a full moon over Dallas you could see her circling the city on her broom! One Sunday after church, we finished a conversation with this woman as pleasantly as we could. We then got into our van to go home. Charlotte and I are the parents of four sons, the oldest two being twins. One of the twins (they were probably eight or nine years old) came up front as we were about to leave and said, "Daddy, you know that lady you and mama were talking to? She scares me."

I started to say, "She scares me, too!" But I didn't. I did the proper daddy thing and said, "Oh? Why does she scare you?"

His answer: "Well, she smiles with her face, but she has real mean eyes."

Eyes sometimes speak louder than our words, don't they? Shulammite smiled not just with her face. She also smiled with her eyes. Solomon admired and was captivated by her attractiveness, by her beauty on the outside as well as her beauty on the inside. Eyes are, after all, windows into the soul.

Shulammite now returns the favor of her man's compliment. It is given willingly and honestly. "How handsome you are, my love. How delightful!" The word *handsome* is the same word as "beautiful" in verse 15, except it is in the masculine gender. "The word occurs 14 times in the Song, but only this once in the masculine form."[4] There is an intensity in her words of praise. She continues by saying he is "delightful." He calms her spirit. He puts her at rest. He sets her heart at peace.

The kindness of his words in verse 15 were thoughtful. They met her at her point of need, and they spoke to her heart. The words were important. The man behind the words is essential. A woman is impressed by a man who understands and respects her personal and emotional needs. She loves a man who talks, who communicates. She is attracted to a man who in strength and masculinity says to her, "You have first place in my affections." She will respond with enthusiasm and energy to a man who treats her in this way.

ACKNOWLEDGE THEIR THOUGHTFULNESS (VV. 16–17)

Shulammite continues her praise of Solomon by pointing out "our bed is lush with foliage; the beams of our houses are cedars, and our rafters are cypresses." Three times the word "our" occurs. His thoughtfulness in preparing a home for them is a source of security. No wonder her eyes speak tranquility and peace. John Snaith notes interestingly, "*Our couch* [bed] denotes in Amos 6:4 particularly stylish and magnificent couches used for feasting; so the couch here . . . is not . . . any old bed!"[5] Solomon's thoughtfulness has provided a strong, sturdy (even royal) home. Their home will be safe and secure, a responsibility God expects a man to bear. It will also be sexual and sensual. "The bed is lush with foliage." It is alive, fresh, fruitful. It will be a place of activity and growth, an environment conducive for the passionate lovemaking God says is a good thing in the marriage bed. Solomon is no insensitive male,

and Shulammite appreciates and acknowledges his thoughtfulness. He will discover his actions are well worth the effort.

AFFIRM THEIR UNIQUENESS (chapter 2, vv. 1–2)

Shulammite sees herself as the "rose of Sharon, a lily of the
valleys." Solomon then adds, "Like a lily among thorns, so is my
darling among the young women." This woman is utterly unique,
rare and special to Solomon. His words have lifted her heart and
self-worth to new heights. "The battle of praise" continues. "Rose
of Sharon" is more accurately "a wild autumn flower of the
valley."[6] Sharon is the low coastal plain which stretches from
Mt. Carmel to the Egyptian border. Wild flowers grew in great
abundance here. "Lily of the valleys" may refer to a lovely white
blossom with six leaves and six petals. "This flower was especially
associated with nuptial occasions."[7] Shulammite, because of
Solomon's praise, sees herself as a beautiful wild flower, free and
untamed by any gardener. She is unique and uniquely Solomon's.
She possesses a natural beauty and a natural desire for her man.
No one has cultivated this unpicked flower. That is an assignment
and privilege reserved for her husband and him alone.

Solomon's statement that she is "like a lily among thorns" only
reinforces the imagery of uniqueness. Shulammite is not just a
flower among many flowers; she is a lily, a beautiful wild flower
amidst thorns. She is a flower. All other women are thorns. By
comparison other women bring pain and are totally undesirable.
Shulammite is his love. She is like an only flower in a world of
thorny weeds. Such praise will not cause other women to applaud
him. It will, however, cause his love to adore him. There is not
another like her as far as he is concerned. This is how to fan the
flames of love.

Like an apricot tree among the trees of the forest,
so is my love among the young men.
I delight to sit in his shade,
and his fruit is sweet to my taste. (v. 3)

PROCLAIM THEIR PROVISION (V. 3)

Verse three is specific and it is sensual. The passion of love is running full throttle. Solomon has told Shulammite some of the real joys she brings to him and how she is the only woman in his life. The confidence she feels in their relationship frees her to give herself even more in unreserved abandonment. Solomon has created a romantic atmosphere. He has built his bride up by focusing on her positive features and gifts. Her response is nothing short of awesome.

TELL OTHERS HOW THEY PROTECT YOU

An apricot or apple tree in the woods would be rare and something you would not expect to find. It, of course, would be sweet to the taste and would provide needed sustenance. Solomon said she was a flower woman among thorny women. Shulammite says that Solomon is a special tree amidst common woods. Finding him brought her "great delight," and she decides to sit down in his shade. She delights in him. She is comforted by him. She is protected by him and only him as never before. "I never knew love before, then came you" could be the song of Shulammite's heart.

TELL OTHERS HOW THEY PLEASE YOU

Apples were believed by some in the ancient world to have sensual and erotic qualities. Shulammite is secure and safe in

Solomon's shade, his watchcare. She now longs for physical intimacy, for lovemaking and sexual union. She simply says, "His fruit
is sweet to my taste." The language is chaste and appropriate. It is
not lewd or out of bounds. It is also highly suggestive and erotic.
What I find in him I like. What I taste, smell, and feel is sweet and
causes me to want more and more.[8] Romance truly is an environment which prepares us for sexual union. As they anticipate their
wedding night (4:1–5:1), the flames of passion are under control
but burning. Is God really in favor of what is ahead? Absolutely!

In fact, God has given us some biblical principles governing
sex. Given that our text anticipates the issue, let us consider some
good guidelines given by a good God.

1. Sexual relations within marriage are holy and good. God
    encourages intimate relations and even warns against
    their cessation (1 Cor. 7:5).
2. Pleasure in sexual relations is both healthy and expected
    (the bodies of both parties belong to the other) (Prov.
    5:15–19; 1 Cor. 7:4).
3. Sexual pleasure is to be guided by the principle that one's
    sexuality is to be other-oriented ("rights" over one's body
    are given in marriage to the other party) (Phil. 2:3–4).
4. Sexual relations are to be regular and normal. No exact
    number of times per week is right or correct, but the bib-
    lical principle is that both parties are to provide adequate
    sexual satisfaction so that both "burning" (sexual desire)
    and temptation to find satisfaction elsewhere are avoided
    (1 Cor. 7:9).
5. The principle of satisfaction means that each party is to
    provide sexual enjoyment (which is "due" him or her in

marriage) as frequently as the other party requires. Other biblical principles (moderation, seeking to please another rather than oneself, etc.) also come into play. Consideration of one's mate is to guide one's requests for sexual relations.

6. In accordance with the principle of "rights," there is to be no sexual bargaining between married persons ("I'll not have relations unless you . . ."). Neither party has the right to make such bargains. This is a form of "marital prostitution" and must be avoided.

7. Sexual relations are equal and reciprocal. The Bible does not give the man superior rights over the woman or the woman superior rights over the man. Mutual stimulation and mutual initiation of relations are legitimate.

8. Whatever is safe, pleasing, enjoyable, and satisfying to both is acceptable. The *body* of each belongs to the other (1 Cor. 7:4). Neither should demand from the other what is painful, harmful, degrading, or distasteful to him or her.

He brought me to the banquet hall,
    and he looked on me with love.
Sustain me with raisins;
    refresh me with apricots,
    for I am lovesick.
His left hand is under my head,
    and his right hand embraces me.
Young women of Jerusalem, I charge you,
    by the gazelles and by the wild does of the field:
    do not stir up or awaken love
    until the appropriate time. (vv. 4–7)

PREPARE FOR PASSION (VV. 4–7)

These verses continue the theme of romance. Interestingly, there is both encouragement and warning. Sex is a powerful gift. It is intoxicating. It has unbelievable potential for good or evil, to build up or tear down, to delight or destroy. Solomon gives us some additional instruction to ensure maximum sex, maximum safety, and maximum satisfaction. This is the sex God has planned from the beginning.

MAKE LOVE IN THE RIGHT PLACE (V. 4)

The man takes his bride into "the banqueting hall," literally "the house of wine." This scene anticipates the wedding night and the marriage bed. The open vineyard with all its beauty and encouragement to love may be in view. Regardless, it will be a place reserved only and exclusively for them. The imagery of wine again speaks of the intoxicating love they will share.

MAKE LOVE WITH THE RIGHT COMMITMENT (V. 4)

"He looked on me with love" speaks of the protective love of her lover, and the safe place to which he has brought her. It also testifies that the love which the king has for her is evident to everyone. He does not say one thing to her in private and contradict that in public. He is not warm and considerate when they are alone but cold and sarcastic when they are with others. He is not ashamed of his love for her. He is glad for all to see. No wonder she grows more and more secure in his love. Carr notes that some translate the Hebrew text, which is admittedly difficult at this point, in a way that is even more strikingly sensual: "And his wish regarding me was love-making" or more simply "his intentions were to make love."[9] Solomon wants her and she wants him. They are the right partners. They have the right passion. They have the right place. But all the essential ingredients are still not present.

MAKE LOVE IN THE RIGHT WAY (VV. 5–6)

Shulammite says she is in the midst of a great feast and she thinks about their lovemaking. Her mind carries her away to the joys of marriage which are just around the corner. The Bible teaches that we should feast on our mate and that God smiles when we do. Shulammite is so overcome with the passion of the moment she feels faint. "For I am lovesick" is translated in the NIV as "I am faint with love." The "I" is emphatic. "I myself am swooning in the rapture of the moment." Does she wish to bail out and bring all of this to a sudden halt? Oh no! On the contrary, she asks for raisins and apricots to strengthen and restore her that she might enjoy more. "Sustain" and "refresh" are imperatives. She demands the necessary nourishment she needs to continue in the passion of their lovemaking. Raisins and apricots both were viewed as highly erotic and sensual. There is no question of the intent or intensity of her desire. One can hardly imagine the reciprocal response all of this would have brought about on the part of Solomon.

In the passion of their love, Shulammite has not lost sight or sense of the warmth, intimacy, and security of their relationship. With one hand he cradles her head. With the other he holds and caresses her. It is interesting to note that the word "embrace" is used in the Old Testament "both of a friendly greeting (Gen. 48:10) and of sexual union (Prov. 5:20)."[10] He is her friend and her lover. Both are important to her. Both are important to all women. No man should ever forget this.

MAKE LOVE AT THE RIGHT TIME (V. 7)

Sexual relationships should take place at the right place with the right person in the right way at the right time. Not just any time is a good time. There is indeed a proper time, a God time. Verse 7 is a recurring theme in the Song (cf. 3:5; 8:4), and its repetition underlines its importance. So crucial is it that it takes the form of an oath. The word "charge" means to adjure or urge. Shulammite is directing her words to the sorority of females (daughters of Jerusalem) as she warns them to pursue passion at the proper pace. The "gazelles" and "wild does" were both beautiful female animals, vigorous and sexually active in season. She understands that though men are usually viewed as the more sexually active and interested, God created women as sexual beings with sexual desires too.

All of us are susceptible to our passions getting out of control, overriding both our reason and will and causing massive hurt and damage. We must understand and understand well: God gave us sex as a wonderful gift to be enjoyed between a man and a woman within the bonds of marriage. This plan of His will never change. He gave us such a plan not to "rain on our parade" or "steal our fun." He gave us this plan because it brings Him glory and it is for our good. Therefore Shulammite warns us, "Do not stir up or awaken love until the appropriate time." Passion is great when the place for its expression is the marriage bed. Duane Garrett says it well, "The girls should not allow themselves to be aroused sexually until the proper time and person arrives. The natural joy of sexual awakening is ruined by premature experimentation."[11]

Maximum sex is marriage sex. The best sex is believers' sex. Why? Because through a relationship with Jesus Christ, you see sex as one of the most beautiful aspects of life. You come to understand that it is more enjoyable to give than to receive, that bodily pleasure can also be spiritual, that men and women have equal rights to sexual pleasure, and that the quality of a sexual relationship is more than just physical pleasure, but it is not less than physical pleasure. God has given us a great gift. Let us enjoy it as He designed it. You will find the delights to be greater than you ever imagined.

THINKING ABOUT SEX

If only because one of them is a man and the other a woman, married couples usually have different attitudes and approaches to sex. Furthermore, many people may come to marriage with varying beliefs and expectations. This attitude assessment tool is designed to open up discussion about these differences. Take it with your partner and see what you can learn about each other.

Agree	Disagree	Uncertain	
_____	_____	_____	Sex is one of the most beautiful aspects of life.
_____	_____	_____	It is more enjoyable to give than to receive.
_____	_____	_____	Bodily pleasure is fleshly and not spiritual.
_____	_____	_____	Sexual intercourse is primarily for physical release.
_____	_____	_____	Our religious beliefs have the greatest influence on our attitudes toward sexual behavior.
_____	_____	_____	Men and women have equal rights to sexual pleasure.

Agree	Disagree	Uncertain	
_____	_____	_____	There are sexual activities that I would consider wrong for a married couple to practice. If you agree, list these: _____

_____

_____

_____

_____	_____	_____	To be truly satisfying, intercourse must lead to simultaneous orgasm.
_____	_____	_____	Sexual fantasies are normal.
_____	_____	_____	Masturbation (self-stimulation) is an acceptable means for sexual pleasure and release.
_____	_____	_____	The male always should be the aggressor in sexual activity.
_____	_____	_____	In general women don't enjoy sex as much as men.
_____	_____	_____	Men should be allowed more freedom in sexual behavior than women.
_____	_____	_____	The quality of a sexual relationship is more than just physical pleasure.

Adapted from Clifford and Joyce Penner, *Sexual Fulfillment in Marriage: A Multimedia Learning Kit,* (Pasadena: Family Concern, Inc., 1977). Available through the Penners at 2 N. Lake Avenue, Suite 610, Pasadena, California 91101.

Chapter 4

Men Are from Earth and Women Are from Earth . . . Deal with It!

THE SONG OF SONGS 2:15

Catch the foxes for us—
   the little foxes that ruin the vineyards—
   for our vineyards are in bloom. (v. 15)

John Gray became a household name and an overnight millionaire with his best-seller *Men Are from Mars, Women Are from Venus.* He has also authored *Mars and Venus in the Bedroom: A Guide to Lasting Romance and Passion; Mars and Venus Together Forever: Relationship Skills for Lasting Love; Mars and Venus in Love; Men, Women and Relationships;* and *What Your Mother Couldn't Tell You and Your Father Didn't Know.* In his books he struck a cord that resonates in each of us. Men and women really are different. We *think* differently; we *see* things differently; we *feel* things differently. We are different and different by *design:* it is the way God made us and the way God intended. He did make us male and female and declared it a good thing (Gen. 1:27). However, John Gray in making his argument did not get it exactly correct. Men are not from Mars, and women are not from Venus. Men are from Earth, and women are from Earth, and we have to deal with it if we are going to make marriage, sex, and romance work. Most marriages that get in trouble do so not over the big things but over the little things. These little things are often grounded in male-female differences. We do sweat the small stuff.

Dorthy Rosby in an article entitled "It's Living Together That Makes Marriage Difficult" tells the story of the woman who shot her husband because he ate her chocolate. She writes, "I probably read about that incident with a Hershey bar in my hand. At the time, I may have even thought he had it coming. But now that I think about it, even I, a confirmed chocoholic, think shooting was extreme." She then adds:

> It truly is the little things that destroy relationships.
> Margarine, chocolate, nylons on the towel rack, hair in
> the sink. I once heard about a couple who fought for
> more than four hours—over a rubber band. He had it,
> and she wanted it. . . . It's the little things that happen
> when you're living together. . . . Part of the problem is
> that God made opposites attract: savers marry
> spenders; neatniks pair up with slobs; and early birds
> team up with night owls. Opposing idiosyncrasies
> come together like weather fronts when couples live
> together.[1]

Dorthy Rosby is right. It is the little things, what Solomon describes as the "little foxes," that can sneak into our relationships and do serious damage. Quietly, unnoticed, and yet effectively, they destroy the tender fabric, the tender vines and grapes of our relationships, whose health is essential for a happy and satisfying marriage.

I want to warn you about two little foxes in particular that are especially dangerous. One I call "the fox of *danger*," and the other I call "the fox of *differences.*"

BEWARE OF THE DANGERS TO YOUR MARRIAGE

The word *catch* in verse 15 is an imperative, a word of command. God issues a strong word about this danger to our relationship. The little foxes are unwelcome intruders who sneak into a marriage and who can destroy the purity of our love and the pricelessness of our relationship. A healthy and happy marriage must be protected. We must be on guard and catch anything that could harm the tender and vulnerable union we have established. Now a question naturally presents itself: What do these little foxes look like? Let me quickly note seven warning signs of a failing marriage.

THE FOX OF ROLE REVERSAL

Warning 1: A marriage will get into trouble when God's role for the husband and the wife is reversed or abused.

God made men to be men, husbands, and fathers. A man should never apologize for being a man, for being a masculine human being. God made women to be women, wives, and mothers. No woman should ever apologize for being a feminine person. You see, no one is as good at being a man as a man, and no one is as good at being a woman as a woman. However, there is great confusion about gender roles today, and men especially are suffering an identity crisis. In our day men struggle with their maleness.

I believe the *South China Post* got it right when it said, "What a real man needs is another man to talk to and reinforce his maleness and help him be a better husband . . . without such a friend, men risk reverting to a mother-child relationship with a spouse." Dr. Peter Karl states, "Men become helpless and insecure and increasingly revert to the classic overgrown kid who expects to be mothered . . . men have few positive role models. Often, they don't even have a good relationship with their fathers, much less any other man."[2]

In preparing for marriage a wise man will look to an older, wiser, and successful husband and father for mentoring. A wise woman will look to another woman for the same kind of guidance and direction. Letting a mature, successfully married couple provide a role model will go a long way toward capturing the little fox of role reversal (see Titus 2:1–8).

THE FOX OF INTIMACY STAGNATION

Warning 2: A marriage will get into trouble when initial, sensual love fails to develop into true intimacy.

Charlotte and I married when I was twenty-one and she was nineteen. Being transparently honest, let me tell you why I married her. She looked good and smelled good and was fun to hold, hug, kiss, and play with. I discovered she was also a really good cook and housekeeper. She had a pleasant personality, and it seemed to me that she would take good care of me for a long time.

Now some of you might say, "You sure are self-centered. I can't believe those were the things you were thinking about when you thought about getting married." Well, before you take me out to be tarred and feathered, let me ask a question, "Why did you marry your mate?"

Let me pick on us guys for a minute. Did you, when looking for a mate, say, "I am going to marry an ugly woman. I want one who always has a partly cloudy disposition with thunderstorms on the horizon. I want one who is no fun to hug and kiss. I want one who can't cook or keep house and shows no potential for change. In short, I'm looking for a mate who will make me miserable the rest of my life." No, I doubt this was the approach taken by any man. Being honest, you probably married, or are considering marriage, for pretty much the same reasons I did.

So what's the point? Am I saying that I did not love Charlotte when we married? Not at all! I did love her—as well as a twenty-one-year-old *boy* can love anything. Now, however, I am a forty-something man (Charlotte says I'm still pretty much a boy in the way I act), and I must tell you, what I feel and know in my heart and soul for Charlotte is so much deeper and precious, it is almost illegitimate to use the word *love* again. Yes, I loved her at twenty-one. But I passionately and intimately love her now. Emotional love got us started, but a soul love has kept us going. We cannot stay where we started in our love relationship. It must grow from day one, or the fox of stagnation will sneak in and do its destructive work.

THE FOX OF SILENCE / STONEWALLING

Warning 3: A marriage will get into trouble when it is not being nourished by regular and genuine communication.

For a marriage to be healthy and vibrant, five areas require consistent attention: (1) *communication,* (2) *finances,* (3) *sex,* (4) *children,* and (5) *in-law relationships.* If any of the latter four are troubled, mark it down; communication broke down. To walk together for a lifetime requires that we talk on a regular basis.

From serious conversations to general chitchat, we must connect verbally if our marriage is going to do well. A wise person said it well, "A courtship begins when a man whispers sweet nothings and ends when he says nothing sweet."

THE FOX OF TIME ILL SPENT

Warning 4: A marriage will get into trouble when forces or persons outside the marriage encroach on the all-important time the two of you need alone to build and maintain a healthy relationship.

Love is a beautiful four-letter word. Sometimes it is best spelled TIME. A marriage is headed for hard times if our best time is given to things that promise only a small return on our investment.

I'm not a hunter. But I have many friends who delight in such foolishness. To be honest, I don't think their elevator reaches the penthouse, if you know what I mean. Let's think about it for a minute. Here is a guy with two options. Option 1: He can, at 4:00 A.M., climb up into a tree in a contraption called a deer stand and freeze while waiting to shoot Bambi. Option 2: He can be back home in a nice warm bed holding his woman. This is a no-brainer as far as I can tell! Now let me be fair. I'm not against hunting, fishing, or many other good things men and women do. What I am against is our giving our best time and quantity time to things that really do not matter. And there is a new fox in the woods who is doing some serious damage in this area. It is called the Internet.

An article entitled, "Spouses Browse Infidelity Online," reported that "the Internet is becoming a breeding ground for adultery, say experts who track the pattern of extramarital affairs. And even stay-at-home moms, who don't get to meet possible partners at work, can be seduced."

"I predict [one] role of the internet in the future will be as a source of affairs," says Peggy Vaughan, author of the *Monogamy Myth*. "Stay-at-home moms in chat rooms are sharing all this personal stuff they are hiding from their partners," Vaughan says. The intensity of women's online relationships can "quickly escalate into their thinking they have found a soulmate. It is so predictable, it is like a script." Vaughan says she knows of women "who have left their marriages before they have even met" their new partners in person.

Shirley Glass has researched "extramarital attachments" since 1975. She warns of online relationships that go over the line. They can become so intense that they threaten marriages, even if there is no sex involved, she says. Such online liaisons involve the three elements of an emotional affair: *secrecy, intimacy, and sexual chemistry.*

Glass cautions: "Discuss your online friendships with your spouse and show him or her your e-mail if your partner is interested. Invite your spouse to join in your correspondence so your internet friend won't get any wrong ideas. And don't exchange sexual fantasies online."[3]

Be careful with whom and where you spend your time. It is a sure sign of where your heart is.

THE FOX OF OUTSIDE INTERFERENCE

Warning 5: A marriage will get into trouble when real and personal needs are being met more and more outside the marriage.

Men and women have basic needs built into the very fabric of their being. For example, a man needs admiration and sexual fulfillment from his wife. A woman needs affection and intimate conversation from her husband. When we are not receiving these things from our mate, we can be tempted to look for them from another person. This is what opens the door for an affair. It comes about slowly, over time, almost without notice. It is one of the most lethal of the foxes that prey on our vineyards. If it comes about that your needs are not being met by your spouse, then go to Jesus. As a Christian, claim Philippians 4:13, "I am able to do all things through Him who strengthens me."

THE FOX OF FATIGUE

Warning 6: A marriage will get into trouble if the wedding vows are considered conditional, marriage is no longer considered a sacred covenant before God, and divorce begins to be considered as a possible solution to an unhappy situation.

While we were living in North Carolina, my middle son, Paul, came home from school one day and asked me a surprising question. "Daddy, do you think you and Mom will ever get a divorce?"

I asked Paul why he asked me such a question. He told me that a friend of his who is always happy and talkative had come to school that day silent and sad. He told me that he saw tears in his eyes and that sometime during the morning the school counselor came and got him and he went home. Paul said he found out at lunch from another friend that the night before his Daddy had left and his mother said they were getting a divorce and that his Dad would not be coming home anymore.

This little boy could not hide his broken heart, and Paul had noticed it. The thought of his own mom and dad splitting up began to run through his mind, and so he had decided to come home and ask me straight out if such a possibility was on our horizon. I quickly informed Paul that no, his Mom and Dad were never going to get a divorce. When we married, we meant it when we said "till death do us part."

That incident reinforced in my mind how important it is for a mom and a dad to stay together and to do their best to make their marriage work. Once we begin to entertain the idea that this relationship is conditional, contingent upon my happiness, and that divorce can be used at any point as an escape hatch, our marriage is moving into dangerous, even deadly waters. Humans are prone to take the easy way out, and divorce is an easier way than putting in the hard work necessary to maintain a healthy marriage.

THE FOX OF MISUNDERSTANDING

Warning 7: A marriage will get into trouble if the man and woman fail to understand and appreciate and enjoy just how really different they are from each other.

This fox leads us into our second major category of foxes, that is the "fox of differences." Let's begin by having a little fun.

I have often said men are like dogs and women are like cats, and I have good evidence for this assertion. Think about it. A man is like a dog. If you feed him, scratch his head, and play with him on a regular basis, you will have a happy man. On the other hand a woman is far more complex and mysterious, much like a cat. A cat can walk into a room, and you look at it and it looks at you. It walks over to you and begins to purr and rub up against your leg in a sweet and gentle fashion. The cat then quickly turns around and walks out of the room, and you say, "That was a really sweet cat."

A few minutes later that same cat walks into the room; you look at it, and it looks at you. Suddenly without provocation or warning, the cat leaps for your face attempting to claw out your eyeballs! Now that was the same cat that came in so sweet and gentle a few moments ago. Something happened while that cat was out of the room. You have no idea what it was, but it certainly changed the disposition of that cat in a matter of seconds. I do see some significant similarities between a cat and a woman!

A friend of mine heard me draw this analogy some years ago, and he sent me something that reinforced and added additional supporting evidence to my thesis that men are dogs and women are cats.

Is it a cat? Is it a woman? Maybe it's both! Why?
1. They do what they want.
2. They rarely listen to you.
3. They're totally unpredictable.
4. They whine when they are not happy.
5. When you want to play, they want to be alone.
6. When you want to be alone, they want to play.
7. They expect you to cater to their every whim.
8. They're moody.
9. They can drive you nuts and cost you an arm and a leg.
10. They leave hair everywhere.

Conclusion: Cats are tiny little women in fur coats.

Is it a dog? Is it a man? Maybe it's both! Why?
1. They lie around all day, sprawled out on the most comfortable piece of furniture in the house.
2. They can hear a package of food opening half a block away, but they can't hear you even when you're in the same room.
3. They leave their toys everywhere.
4. They growl when they are not happy.

5. When you want to play, they want to play.
6. When you want to be left alone, they still want to play.
7. They are great at begging.
8. They will love you forever if you feed them and rub their tummies.
9. They do disgusting things with their mouths and then try to give you a kiss.
10. They can look dumb and lovable all at the same time.

Conclusion: Dogs are tiny little men in fur coats.

Yes, men and women really are different, and they are different in some significant ways. Let me highlight six of them.

1. Communication—Listening is hard work for men, but it brings happiness to women. Men are often intimidated in conversation because we are not nearly as good at it as women are. On the other hand, women find conversation nourishing and meaningful to their heart and soul. Men tend to report facts; women are far more interested in sharing feelings. Men feel compelled to offer solutions; women want affirmation and assurance. Men unfortunately do not respond well to hints; women are subtle and coded in their conversation. The tone of her voice, a glance of her eye, a particular form of body language may speak far louder than the words that are coming from her mouth. Any man who does not pick up on these nonverbal signals will fail at communication and will be a source of frustration to the woman in his life.

2. Romance—Romance for men is a three-letter word: *sex.* For women romance can mean lots of things. It is difficult for men to understand, but for women romance may or may not include sex. Indeed, women find some of the most interesting things romantic—praying with her, helping her wash the dishes, cleaning out the garage, or running a warm bubble bath and lighting a candle. All of these things are strange to a male, but they speak deeply to the heart of a woman.

The simple fact is men and women are wired differently when it comes to the area of romance. For men, romance is highly visual; it is what they see. For women, romance is extremely relational and personal; it is what they feel. Men indeed are creatures of sight; they are moved by what they see. Women on the other hand are creatures of the ear and of the heart; they are moved by what they hear and by what they feel.

This point is so crucial it might be worth our digressing for just a moment. What do men say romance is to them? The following list of fifteen suggestions from Gary Chapman's wonderful book *Toward a Growing Marriage* is not exhaustive, but it is helpful as a woman tries to understand where a man is coming from in this area of romance.

1. Be attractive at bedtime—nothing in the hair or strange on the face. Wear something besides granny gowns and pajamas.
2. Do not be ashamed to show you enjoy being with me.
3. Dress more appealingly when I am at home (no housecoats, slippers, etc.).
4. Do things to catch my attention: remember that a man is easily excited by *sight*.
5. Communicate more openly about sex.
6. Do not make me feel guilty at night for my inconsistencies during the day (such as being affectionate enough).
7. Be more aware of my needs and desires as a man.

8. Show more desire and understand that caressing and foreplay are as important to me as they are to you.

9. Do not allow yourself to remain upset over everyday events that go wrong.

10. Do not try to fake enjoyment. Be authentic in your response to me.

11. Do not try to punish me by denying me sex or by giving it grudgingly.

12. Treat me like your lover.

13. Listen to my suggestions on what you can do to improve our sexual relationship.

14. Forgive me when I fall short of what I should be.

15. Tell me what I can do to be the sexual partner you desire.[4]

On the other hand, what suggestions have wives made to their husbands as to how they can make romance and sexual relations more meaningful? Again, this list is to help us get the idea.

1. Show more affection; give attention throughout the day; come in after work and kiss me on my neck and ask me about my day (and stay around and listen!).

2. Be more sympathetic when I am really sick.

3. Accept me as I am; accept me even when you see the worst side of me.

4. Tell me that you love me at times other than when we are in bed; phone sometimes just to say, "I love you!" Do not be ashamed to tell me, "I love you" in front of others.

5. While I am bathing or showering, find soft music on the radio or dim the lights and light a candle.

6. Honor Christ as the head of our home.

7. Talk to me after our lovemaking; make caresses after our lovemaking and hold me.

8. Be sweet and loving (at least one hour) before initiating sex.

9. Show an interest in what I have to say in the morning.

10. Help me wash dinner dishes and clean the kitchen.

11. Pay romantic attention to me (hold hands, kiss) even during relatively unromantic activities (television watching, car riding, walking in the mall, etc.)

12. Help me feel that I am sexually and romantically attractive by complimenting me more often.

13. Pray with me about the problems and victories you are having; let me express my own needs to you.

14. Do not approach lovemaking as a ritualistic activity; make each time a new experience.

15. Think of something nice to say about me and do it in front of others often.[5]

3. Needs—Women need to feel valued; men need to feel successful. Indeed, if you talk to a man about feeling valued, he probably will not understand what you are getting at. But if you talk to him about his need to feel successful, he will immediately understand what you mean. Women need to be heard. Communication is invaluable in speaking to the heart of a woman. Men, on the other hand, like their canine companions, need to be praised. When a woman praises her man, she speaks to one of the most basic needs of his heart, his need for admiration. His soul soars at the special place he occupies in the evaluation of his spouse.

4. Self-worth—Women value relational moments and fear neglect. Men value occupational achievements and fear failure.

Women are relational creatures. Barbara O'Chester wisely asserts, "Women love to make a memory." Men would not really understand what that is all about. However, men often gauge their own self-worth by what they do for a living. Furthermore, failure at one's occupational assignment can be absolutely devastating to a man's self-worth. If and when a man loses his job, it is an especially crucial time for a woman to step in and affirm him and let him know that she still values him above all other men. We have seen this truth reiterated again and again in the Song of Songs as Shulammite praises Solomon in every imaginable way. A good wife will not forget how important this is to the fragile male ego. Men, on the other hand, must understand that the relationships of life are absolutely crucial to a woman. If a man neglects his wife, he wounds her spirit and bruises her heart in a way that can hardly be healed.

5. *Time*—Men do not think much about time. Women, however, value both quantity and quality of time. Baby boomers have subjected themselves willingly to a great lie. We told ourselves that though we did not give our children quantity time because of the busyness of our schedules, we more than made up for it with quality time. However, we now know that for a child, and for that matter a spouse, quality time is quantity time. Both a spouse and children want you when they want you; and if you're not there, they don't get you. Men in this context tend to go with the flow. We have to be honest; most of us are not very creative. This is a tragedy. Women are thrilled beyond words when their man shows his appreciation for them with specific and creative ideas.

How many times has a man blown it on a date night with his wife? He realizes that it has been some time since he took his wife out for a date, and so he approaches her and says, "Honey, how about a date this Friday night?" She, of course, passes out, and he is forced to call 911 to have emergency service to revive her! However, once she has regained consciousness, she quickly responds with an enthusiastic yes!

She then asks the question that has been building within her soul since she heard her husband's offer, "What are we going to do?" Then tragically and shamefully there comes out of the mouth of a male perhaps some of the dumbest words that have ever been uttered by human lips, "Oh, it doesn't matter to me."

When a man utters those words, he basically crushes the heart of his wife, and he destroys any possibility for good that could have come out of a romantic rendezvous the coming weekend. A wise man will not only invite his wife out for a date; he will also be creative and specific in planning out the entire event (including taking care of the baby-sitter!). The bottom line is this: tell me where you spend your time, and I will tell you what you love.

Reba McEntire, a country singer, recorded a song several years ago written by Richard Leigh and Layng Martine, Jr. It could tragically be the theme song of many a little boy or little girl as they reflect on this issue of time as it relates to their daddy.

The Greatest Man

The greatest man I never knew
Lived just down the hall
And everyday we said hello
But never touched at all.
He was in his paper.
I was in my room
How was I to know he thought I hung the moon?

The greatest man I never knew
Came home late every night
He never had too much to say
Too much was on his mind.
I never really knew him,
And now it seems so sad.
Everything he gave to us took all he had.

Then the days turned into years,
And the memories to black and white.
He grew cold like an old winter wind
Blowing across my life.

The greatest words I never heard
I guess I'll never hear.
The man I thought could never die
Been dead almost a year.
He was good at business,
But there was business left to do.
He never said he loved me, guess he thought I knew.[6]

6. Parenting—God designed mothers to nurture and provide the emotional support that is necessary for the healthy development of a child. Fathers provide strength and a child's sense of self-worth and security. Amazingly, even the simple presence of the man in the home can make a tremendous impact on the life of a child. That's why the death of a father is hurtful. But the loss of a father by divorce is utterly tragic. One of my favorite theologians is Erma Bombeck! In her book *Family—the Ties That Bind . . . and Gag!* she illustrates beautifully the importance that the presence of a father can make in the life of a child.

One morning my father didn't get up and go to work.
He went to the hospital and died the next day. I hadn't
thought that much about him before. He was just
someone who left and came home and seemed glad to
see everyone at night. He opened the jar of pickles
when no one else could. He was the only one in the
house who wasn't afraid to go into the basement by
himself. He cut himself shaving, but no one kissed it or
got excited about it. It was understood when it rained,
he got the car and brought it around to the door.
When anyone was sick, he went to get the prescription
filled. He took lots of pictures . . . but he was never in
them. Whenever I played house, the Mother doll had a
lot to do. I never knew what to do with the Daddy doll,
so I had him say, "I'm going off to work now" and
threw him under the bed. The funeral was in our living
room and a lot of people came and brought all kinds
of good food and cakes. We had never had so much
company before. I went to my room and felt under the
bed for the Daddy doll. When I found him, I dusted
him off and put him on my bed. He never did anything. I didn't know his leaving would hurt so much.[7]

Yes, daddies are important to the well-being of their children,
but so are their mothers. We live in a day when motherhood is not
held in the high esteem that it once was. Unfortunately, many
women have mistakenly sacrificed the gift of motherhood and the
joy of childbearing for career and other enticements that in the
long run will never deliver the joy and blessings that rearing children provides.

Several years ago someone sent me an article one woman speaking to another. I doubt I have ever read anything that seemed to capture in such a powerful fashion the greatness and importance of motherhood. I think every woman who reads these words will probably need a tissue at the end of the story.

It Will Change Your Life

Time is running out for my friend. While we are sitting at lunch, she casually mentions that she and her husband are thinking of "starting a family." What she means is that her biological clock has begun its countdown, and she is being forced to consider the prospect of motherhood.

"We're taking a survey," she says half joking. "Do you think I should have a baby?"

"It will change your life," I say carefully, keeping my tone neutral.

"I know," she says. "No more spontaneous vacations . . . "

But that is not what I mean at all, and I try to decide what to tell her. I want her to know what she will never learn in childbirth classes: that the physical wounds of childbearing heal, but that becoming a mother will leave an emotional wound so raw that she will be forever vulnerable. I consider warning her that she will never read a newspaper again without asking "What if that had been my child?" That every plane crash, every fire will haunt her. That when she sees pictures of starving children, she will wonder if anything could be worse than watching your child die.

I look at her manicured nails and stylish suit and think that no matter how sophisticated she is, becoming a mother will reduce her to the primitive level of a bear protecting her cub. That an urgent call of "MOM!" will cause her to drop her best crystal without a moment's hesitation.

I feel I should warn her that no matter how many years she has invested in her career, she will be professionally derailed by motherhood. Oh, she might arrange for childcare, but one day she will be going into an important business meeting, and she will think about her baby's sweet smell. She will have to use every ounce of discipline to keep from running home, just to make sure her child is all right. I want my friend to know that every day decisions will no longer be routine. That a 5-year-old boy's desire to go to the men's restroom rather than the women's at a restaurant will become a major dilemma. That issues of independence and gender identity will be weighed against the prospect that a child molester may be lurking in that men's restroom. However decisive she may be at the office, she will second-guess herself constantly as a mother.

Looking at my attractive friend, I want to assure her that eventually she will shed the pounds of pregnancy, but she will never feel the same about herself. That her life now, so important, will be of less value to her once she has a child. That she would give it up in a moment to save her offspring, but will also hope for more years—not to accomplish her own dreams, but to watch her child accomplish his.

My friend's relationship with her husband will
change, but not in the ways she thinks. I wish she
could understand how much more you can love a man
who is always careful to powder the baby or who never
hesitates to play with his son or daughter. I think she
should know that she will fall in love with her husband
all over again, but for reasons she would now find very
unromantic. I want to describe to my friend the exhilaration of seeing your child learn to hit a baseball.
I want to capture for her the belly laugh of a baby who
is touching the soft fur of a dog for the first time. I
want her to taste the joy that is so real it hurts.

   My friend's quizzical look makes me realize that
tears have formed in my eyes. "You'll never regret it,"
I finally say. Then squeezing my friend's hand, I offer a
prayer for her and me and all the mere mortal women
who stumble their way into this holiest of callings.[8]

Several years ago I was doing a family life conference in
south Florida. I had talked about the fact that a mother really
does become something of a bear protecting her cub whenever
her children are in trouble. After the conference a man came up
to me and said, "What you said this morning is absolutely the
truth. Let me tell you what happened down here recently." He
then relayed to me the story of a family that was in their backyard down in the Everglades. While they were out playing and
doing things, an alligator came up out of the bush and grabbed
their small child and began to run back into the bush toward
the water. The father and mother both saw what was happening.
The father, being the typical male, quickly looked for something

that he might grab as a weapon to go and attack the alligator. The mother, however, looked for nothing. She immediately went into a sprint, leaped upon the alligator, and began to bite it, hit it, kick it, and scream at it. Finally, bruised and battered, the alligator let go of the small child and made its way quickly back into the safety of the water! The mother stood up, realized what she had just done, and immediately passed out there in the backyard!

Why did she do this? Because being the woman, she began with her heart not her head, as did her husband. Whenever a child is in danger and both parents see it, almost always the mother will react more quickly. Why? Does she love the child more? I don't think so. Men start with the head and then move to the heart. This takes a bit longer. Women on the other hand start with the heart and move to the head. This takes no time at all.

If we are to beat the little foxes, we must recognize that this is a fight that will have to take place on a day-by-day basis. The victories of yesterday will not be sufficient for the battles of tomorrow. It is absolutely essential that we grow a little bit every day in our relationship with each other.

Several years ago Harry Chapin wrote a song entitled, "We Grew Up a Little Bit." Harry Chapin was a ballad singer. He did not have many answers, but he sure knew how to raise the right questions. Read the words of this song, and see if they will not challenge your heart and your commitment to each other, to grow at least a little bit every single day in this wonderful relationship we call marriage.

We Grew Up a Little Bit
We got married early and just a little bit late.
Baby came too early, but some things just can't wait.

We were just beginning but it was very clear
We grew up a little bit that year.

I caught on as a meter man. You were caught at home.
When I started night school you ended up alone.
But you had another baby while I had my career.
And we grew up a little bit. We grew up a little bit.
We grew up a little bit that year.

They put me in an office job, the young man on the
    move.
We bought a house in Shaker Heights. You supervised
    the move.
We were cashing checks. You were changing children
    while I played engineer.
And we were growing ever faster every year.

But I got bored of kilowatts and you were tired of kids.
I started staying out at night, and soon that's what you
    did.
At parties we'd go separately. You'd wiggle and I'd leer.
And we were growing faster. We were growing ever faster.
We were growing ever faster every year.

Well you learned to live in silence. I learned to live in lies.
And we both ignored the empty spaces growing in our
    eyes.
Your breath became a gin and tonic while mine
    became a beer.
And we grew up a little more last year.

Today at work they passed me by and promoted John
    instead.
I came home to find you'd wrecked the car. I guess I
    lost my head.
Well, I can't believe I hit you but the rage came on so
    strong.
Ah, where did we go wrong?

As you sit there crying I wonder who you are?
The partner-stranger-friend and foe who's come with
me this far.
We stand here in the ashes and I guess it is quite clear.
We did not really grow too much each year.

So, you say we're going nowhere. Well, I know that's
where we've been.
But I still can't help wondering can we begin again?
I feel so full of questions, curiosity and fear.
But could we grow a little bit . . . Could we grow a little
bit . . .
Can we grow a little bit this year?[9]

Yes, men and women are from Earth, and we have to deal with
it. If, however, we can with God's grace, grow a little bit each day,
we can move beyond "dealing with it" to delighting in it. Let's give
it our best and see what God does.

Chapter 5

Making Preparation for Marriage

THE SONG OF SONGS 2:8–17

Several years ago, *USA Today* carried an article from *Men's Health* magazine profiling the average American male. The article was based on "reports, surveys, and reams of marketing data." The report was not encouraging. The study revealed that the average American man:

- Loses his virginity at seventeen.
- Marries at twenty-six.
- Can run a mile, but it takes him twelve minutes.
- Can do only thirty to thirty-three sit-ups per minute.
- Sleeps seven hours a night.
- Buys frozen pizza four times a month.
- Can bench press only eighty-eight percent of his body weight.
- Has seventy to eighty pounds of muscle.
- Watches TV about twenty-eight hours per week.
- Saves less than three thousand dollars per year for retirement.
- Earns an annual salary of $29,533.

- Is 5 feet 9 inches tall and weighs 172 pounds.
- Will have sex with five to ten partners during his lifetime.
- Will consume eleven beers in a seven-day period.

Given this dismal portrait, I am not surprised fewer and fewer women are marrying. We should probably be amazed that they are marrying at all. This guy is not the kind of guy God intended a man to be. He is certainly not the guy we find in the Song of Songs. He is not the guy with whom most women would want to spend a lifetime.

When preparing for marriage, we should gather the facts and learn as much about our potential mate as possible. We need to know the good and the bad. No question is out of bounds or off-limits. If a potential husband or wife holds back information and becomes secretive about various aspects of his or her life, warning bells should start ringing immediately.

I believe God would say there are several crucial questions we should consider before saying, "I do." These questions are simple but probing, and they will help us to understand our future mate and make wise preparation for marriage.

> Listen! My love is approaching.
> Look! Here he comes,
> leaping over the mountains,
> bounding over the hills.
>
> My lover is like a gazelle
> or a young stag.
> Look! He is standing behind our wall,
> gazing through the windows,
> peering through the lattice. (vv. 8–9)

QUESTION 1: ARE THEY TRANSPARENT IN THEIR ACTIONS? (VV. 8–9)

The scene has shifted from the city and the palace back to the country and Shulammite's home. The wedding day of the couple in love is just a few days away. Every word and every action should be carefully weighed right up until the time of the ceremony. One cannot have too much information when it comes to this momentous decision. The most important decision a person will ever make in all of life is whether to trust Jesus Christ as Lord and Savior. The second most important decision is who you will marry. It is possible to have too little information before marriage, and when that happens the results are often tragic. Shulammite is a wise woman. She is a student of Solomon. She watches every move he makes. Is he the real deal? Is it authentic? Are his true intentions apparent? What were the clues she gathered?

WATCH THEIR ACTIONS (VV. 8–9)

Here is a truism: "Actions speak louder than words." When Solomon acted, Shulammite watched, and she liked what she saw. Five times in verses 8–17 she calls Solomon "my love." Both words are important. He is *my* love. He is my *love*. A tender love affair has been growing for some time. Everything seems to be falling into place. The hearts of two lovers are being knit together. Does Shulammite find Solomon's actions to be in concert with what her heart is telling her? Indeed she does. She hears his voice calling out to her as he comes for her. She compliments his agility ("leaping" and "bounding") and his attractiveness ("like a gazelle or a young stag"). His advance is a clear indication of his desire for her and only her. He is enthusiastic. He is aboveboard and open about his love for his lady. He is not ashamed to be public about his affection. He makes this clear as he comes up to the wall of the home. No one is in doubt about his feelings for this lady.

WATCH THEIR EYES (V. 9)

As we noted earlier, "Eyes are windows into the soul." Solomon looks and gazes through the windows and lattice of the house. His eyes speak, and they speak loudly. They make clear his desire for her. He wants her, but he approaches her with honor and respect. He comes close, with loving, penetrating glances, but he will maintain a distance until they unite their lives in marriage. She is more than a sex toy he longs to play with. She is a wonderful lady, deserving his best behavior both now and later. His present actions are a good indication of what his future behavior will be like.

Several years ago I was scheduled to do a family life conference in another state. A week or so before I was to go, I received an anonymous card in the mail from a woman with a broken heart. Here is what she wrote.

> Dear Dr. Akin,
> I hope you receive my card before the marriage conference. . . . I recently married a member of our church. He will be attending your seminar. This past Valentine's Day he did not acknowledge the romantic holiday, and I was very hurt. I watched as my coworkers received flowers. To make things worse, he joked about it in front of one of my friends. My mom told me I should have known what to expect since he never gave me flowers while we were dating. This may sound

selfish and petty on my part. I am just so discouraged!
After I come home from my job, I do all the housework and cooking and shopping. I wouldn't mind so
much if he would just occasionally show his appreciation. The only time he has ever given me a gift is on
my birthday and Christmas. It would mean so much to
me if just once he would give me something just
because he loves me. I exercise and try to look nice.
I iron all his clothes and cook his favorite meals. He
has thousands of dollars to invest in the stock market,
but he has never spent one dollar on a romantic gift
for me. I know flowers will eventually wilt, but they are
so beautiful. I'm afraid my love will eventually wilt.
Will you pray for me?

Wow! What a terrible situation. What an out-of-touch husband. This husband probably loves his wife, but he has no clue
how to show it. In fact, it appears he never has. He was insensitive
before they married, and he is insensitive after they married.
Shouldn't she have seen it coming? We can't criticize the man for
not being transparent. What she saw is what she got. Transparency, you see, is a two-way street. What are they showing? What
are you seeing? We must work at full disclosure on one end and
honest evaluation on the other.

My love calls to me:
Arise, my darling.
Come away, my beautiful one.
For now the winter is past;
the rain has ended and gone away.

The blossoms appear in the countryside.
The time of singing has come,
    and the turtledove's cooing is heard in our land.
The fig tree ripens its figs;
    the blossoming vines give off their fragrance.
Arise, my darling.
    Come away, my beautiful one.
O my dove—in the clefts of the rock,
    in the crevices of the cliff—
    let me see your face,
    let me hear your voice;
    for your voice is sweet,
    and your face is lovely. (2:10–14)

QUESTION 2: ARE THEY TENDER WITH THEIR WORDS? (vv. 10–14)

USA Today, March 30, 2000, reported on a study that found that how we talk, even more than what we say, can predict whether a marriage will succeed or fail.

> How newlyweds talk to each other, more than what they actually say, can predict which couples will divorce with 87% accuracy, new government-sponsored research says.
>
> The results of the 10-year study from the University of Washington, Seattle, add to the growing body of research sponsored by the National Institute of Mental Health that seeks to identify what saves marriages.

Interviewed within six months of marriage,
couples who will endure already see each other
"through rose-colored glasses," study co-author Sybil
Carrere says. "Their behavior toward each other is positive." Those who will divorce already see each other
"through fogged lenses," seeming cynical and unable to
say good things about each other.[1]

How we say things is as important as what we say. A kind attitude and a tender tone will foster receptive ears on the other end.
For the third time Shulammite refers to Solomon as "my love."
With a gentleness and tenderness in his voice, he speaks and she
listens. What kinds of things should we listen for in a potential
mate, a lifelong spouse?

LISTEN FOR PRAISE (VV. 10, 13)

In verses 10 and 13 Solomon invites Shulammite to arise and
come away with him. He is utterly transparent in his intentions.
He is also careful with his words. He calls her his "darling" (NKJV
"love") and his "beautiful one." She is a joy to his heart and to his
eyes. He loves her and he finds her irresistibly beautiful. He does
not keep his thoughts to himself. He does not assume that she
knows how he feels; he tells her how he feels. He gives her public
and specific praise.

LISTEN FOR PARTICULARS (VV. 11–13)

Solomon was an atypical man when it came to romance. He
understood that the way to a woman's heart is often in the
details, the little things. In verses 11–13 Solomon invites

Shulammite to take a walk in the countryside. No doubt she would have found this romantic. Furthermore, the poetic description of the passing of winter and the coming of spring is startling, especially for a man. His attention to detail is a model for all men everywhere.

It is likely that Solomon's elaborate description has a double focus. Springtime is universally thought of as a time for love. Falling in love is like experiencing springtime all over again. Everything is fresh, new, and alive. Things simply look different when you are in love. You see things and notice things that previously you missed or overlooked. For this young couple in love, winter and rain were long gone. Flowers were blooming, birds were singing, spring was in the air. They could *see* it and *smell* it (v. 13). Love could be found anywhere and everywhere they looked or turned.

LISTEN FOR PASSION (V. 14)

When two people are in love, they want to spend time alone, just the two of them. Solomon extends his invitation again, calling Shulammite his "dove" (cf. 1:15). Doves are gentle and beautiful. They often nestle in the crevices of the rock, out of sight and safely hidden. Solomon compares Shulammite to such a dove and urges her to come out to him. She has kept herself safe and secure until God brought the right man into her life. She has saved herself for marriage. Now the right man has arrived, and he asks her to come to him. One senses the passion of his request when he says he desires to see her lovely face and hear her sweet voice. Keel's comments strike home the thrust of Solomon's words, "The voice is just as infatuating (or 'sweet'; cf. Prov. 20:17) as the face is ravishing. . . . The usual translations ('pleasant,' 'lovely,' etc.) are too pallid, failing to do justice to the intensity that enlivens this little song."[2]

Craig Glickman wisely writes:

> One good indication of real love is the desire to communicate, a wish to discover all about this person whom you love so much. No detail seems too trivial to be related. No mood or feeling of one is unimportant to the other. And you care about the details and the feelings because you care so much about the person. That which would be insignificant or boring to even a good friend is eagerly received with genuine interest by the one who loves you. . . . The mere voice of the one loved is enchantingly special just in itself. One could read from the telephone book and the other would raptly listen simply for the sound of the voice.[3]

I remember reading one day about how difficult a time Olympian Al Joyner was having following the unexpected death of his wife Flo-Jo, Florence-Griffith Joyner, the beautiful Olympic track star. He said that he had refused to change their answering machine at home. Why? Because it still contained her voice.

Catch the foxes for us—
    the little foxes that ruin the vineyards—
    for our vineyards are in bloom. (v. 15)

QUESTION 3: ARE THEY TENACIOUS IN THEIR COMMITMENT? (V. 15)

"Foxes were notorious in the ancient world for damaging vineyards. . . . Some ancient sources also suggest that foxes were particularly fond of grapes."[4] Here the "little foxes" represent those dangers and problems that can sneak into a relationship and do untold damage, almost without notice, until it is too late. Even in the best relationship, a couple is vulnerable to potentially destructive problems. Here the proverb is certainly true: "An ounce of prevention is worth a pound of cure." A couple must be determined and tenacious in their commitment to "catch the little foxes." Interestingly, the word *catch* is an imperative, a word of command from the Lord. We should take to heart at least two important truths in this regard.

TROUBLE IS USUALLY IN THE SMALL THINGS

Foxes are little animals, not large ones. You hardly notice them, and they are good at hiding. Only when the damage is done do you even realize they were there. Issues like role responsibilities, conflict resolution, goals, expectations, finances, sex, spiritual compatibility, interpersonal compatibility, social compatibility, and in-law relations do not just naturally work in a relationship. They must be addressed and worked through on an ongoing basis if a marriage is to grow and develop.

RELATIONSHIPS ARE UNIQUELY SENSITIVE

Solomon says, "Our vineyards are in bloom." They are vulnerable to attack, and so is our marriage. We must provide necessary and essential protection. In other words, in actions and attitude we must, with dogged determination, resolve to nurture and tend to our relationships with great care and concern. Any wise couple will consider a number of questions as they contemplate the prospects of marriage. The following questions address several small things that could become big things if not faced head-on.

1. Can you identify a day or time period when you placed your faith in Christ for salvation? (John 1:12; Rom. 10:9–10, 13)
2. Do you have certainty that your partner has come to faith in Christ?
3. Have you discussed and come to agreement on what the Bible means when it says that the husband is to be a loving leader and the wife is to be a submissive helper? (Eph. 5:21–33)
4. Have you agreed always to tell your partner the truth? (Eph. 4:15)
5. Have you committed never to criticize your partner in public?
6. Do you agree on how decisions will be made when disagreement occurs?
7. Are you both committed to intimacy in your communication as a couple and to the effort this will require?
8. Do you both want to be used of God to help your partner come to full maturity as a Christian?
9. Do you like the outlook on life and the values of your partner?
10. Are you personally committed to making your marriage a success whatever the cost or sacrifice?

11. Have you determined premarital sexual standards by open discussion so that each feels that the decision reached honors the Lord? (1 Cor. 6:18–20)

12. Does the wife-to-be realize that men move from the visual to the physical and therefore need a healthy sexual relationship with their spouse to deter temptation?

13. Does the husband-to-be realize that women move from the emotional to the sexual and therefore need love demonstrated often in verbal and practical ways?

14. Do you have complete confidence that your partner will be faithful to you? Could you trust her or him with a member of the opposite sex?

15. Has your partner demonstrated a lifestyle that is similar to yours in spiritual commitment?

16. Have you decided where you will attend church and to what degree you will become involved?

17. Are you comfortable sharing feelings, desires, and goals with your partner?

18. Do you experience a sense of emotional pain when you are separated from your partner?

19. Have you demonstrated a willingness to be flexible in your relationship?

20. Have you been able to forgive your partner for an offense, reconcile, and forget the matter? (Eph. 4:32)

21. Are both sets of parents in agreement with your intentions?

22. Have you objectively looked at your partner's family to see the major influences in shaping her or his life?

23. Do you respect your partner, and are you proud to have people for whom you have high regard meet him or her?

24. Do you find generally that you like the same people?

25. Have you observed differences in your social backgrounds that might cause conflicts?

Dealing with these types of questions will provide a helpful and healthy protection that will make it extremely difficult for those little foxes to do their damage.

My love is mine and I am his;
  he feeds among the lilies.
Before the day breaks
  and the shadows flee,
turn to me, my love, and be like a gazelle
  or a young stag on the divided mountains. (vv. 16–17)

QUESTION 4: ARE THEY TRUSTWORTHY FOR LIFE? (VV. 16–17)

Solomon and Shulammite are realistic about their romance. They love each other, but they also know problems are inevitable. They have an initial strategy for facing difficulties when they arise (v. 15). Still, do they have what it takes to go the distance? Are they serious about the words "till death do us part?" I believe they are, and so must we be. How will I know if he (she) really loves me, and will he (she) love me for life?

YOU MUST KNOW YOU BELONG TO EACH OTHER (V. 16)

A healthy relationship shows confidence and commitment. Each will know of the love and devotion of the other. Shulammite could say with bold assurance "My love is mine and I am his." They enjoy an intimate and exclusive love. Like 90 percent of Americans, they believe extramarital affairs are wrong. However, unlike the 35 percent of women and 45 percent of men who allegedly cheat on their spouses,[5] they are determined to be true to each other. "He feeds among the lilies" indicates that he enjoys the love and pleasures she has to offer. Again, because she is confident of their relationship, she freely gives herself to him. Security is essential to maximum sexual and marital enjoyment.

YOU MUST KNOW YOU WANT EACH OTHER (V. 17)

The couple longs for marital union and sexual consummation. Because they belong to each other, they want each other with no barriers standing in the way. Thinking ahead to what they will enjoy, Shulammite invites Solomon to come unto her with the agility, strength, and beauty of a gazelle or young stag (cf. v. 9). Her invitation includes an episode of all night lovemaking. Would any red-blooded, sane male say no?

The "divided mountains" (NKJV "mountains of Bether") is literally "hills or mountains of separation." This would seem to be a not-so-subtle reference to the woman's breasts (cf. 4:6). With all her desire and passion she welcomes him. "Before the day breaks" (lit. "breathes") "and the shadows flee away" (in other words "all night"), be my lover and enjoy the fruits of our love.

Shulammite has come a long way in her own personal self-evaluation. The unreserved love of this man who has entered her life has effected a great change. She is now the woman God created her to be. Together the two of them are far better and more beautiful than they could have ever been alone. Love will do that when we pursue it God's way and with all our heart.

Norman Wright tells the story of "The 8-Cow Wife." Now

before you wonder if I have lost it (or if he has), just read on and see if God doesn't teach us all something very valuable.

When I married my wife, we both were insecure and she did everything she could to try to please me. I didn't realize how dominating and uncaring I was toward her. My actions in our early marriage caused her to withdraw even more. I wanted her to be self-assured, to hold her head high, and her shoulders back. I wanted her to be feminine and sensual.

The more I wanted her to change, the more withdrawn and insecure she felt. I was causing her to be the opposite of what I wanted her to be. I began to realize the demands I was putting on her, not so much by words but by body language.

By God's grace I learned that I must love the woman I married, not the woman of my fantasies. I made a commitment to love Susan for who she was— who God created her to be.

The change came about in a very interesting way. During a trip to Atlanta I read an article in *Reader's Digest*. I made a copy of it and have kept it in my heart and mind ever since.

It was the story of Johnny Lingo, a man who lived in the South Pacific. The islanders all spoke highly of this man, but when it came time for him to find a wife the people shook their heads in disbelief. In order to obtain a wife you paid for her by giving her father cows. Four to six cows was considered a high price. But the woman Johnny Lingo chose was plain, skinny and

walked with her shoulders hunched and her head
down. She was very hesitant and shy. What surprised
everyone was Johnny's offer—he gave eight cows for
her! Everyone chuckled about it, since they believed his
father-in-law put one over on him.

Several months after the wedding, a visitor from
the U.S. came to the islands to trade and heard the
story about Johnny Lingo and his eight-cow wife.
Upon meeting Johnny and his wife the visitor was
totally taken back, since this wasn't a shy, plain and
hesitant woman but one who was beautiful, poised and
confident. The visitor asked about the transformation,
and Johnny Lingo's response was very simple.
"I wanted an eight-cow woman, and when I paid that
for her and treated her in that fashion, she began to
believe that she was an eight-cow woman. She discovered she was worth more than any other woman in the
islands. And what matters most is what a woman
thinks about herself."[6]

Chapter 6

The Case for Marriage

THE SONG OF SONGS 3:1–5

Marriage is one of the greatest things going. In a recent book entitled *The Case for Marriage,* Linda Waite and Maggie Gallagher argue convincingly, and against a great deal of contemporary "wisdom," that married people are "happier, healthier, and better off financially." Amazing, isn't it? Popular culture is now discovering what many of us already knew. *God knows best!* Yes, even scientific research is now vindicating the Creator's idea of marriage and the family. For example, when we examine evidence on sex, marriage, and children, we discover God knows best.

SEX

In 1993 it was reported that sixty-eight million Americans had a sexually transmitted disease.[1] Approximately 15.3 million Americans contract an STD annually. One in four of the victims is under age twenty. Five of the eleven most commonly reported infectious diseases in this country in 1998, the last year for which data are available, were STDs. And that doesn't include the most common STDs, herpes and human papilloma virus (HPV); the Centers for Disease Control and Prevention (CDC) don't collect data on these. HPV causes over ninety percent of cancer and pre-cancer of the cervix, which, in turn, is causing the deaths of approximately five thousand American women yearly.

The number of lifetime sex partners is highly correlated with the likelihood of contracting an STD. Studies from the CDC clearly show that, on average, the younger a person is when he or she starts to have sex, the more partners he or she is likely to have. Hence, delay sexual activity until marriage and avoid STDs. Furthermore, the likelihood of contracting an STD during marriage is negligible. Thus, more marriage means fewer STDs.[2] And keep this in mind: many STDs are incurable; others can render you sterile; and some are potentially fatal. It is an amazing reality to think that if we would simply do sex God's way, one man with one woman within the covenant of marriage for life, every single STD would disappear from the planet in one generation.

We now know sex is more satisfying for those who wait until marriage. A survey of sexuality, which was called the "most authoritative ever" by *U.S. News & World Report*, conducted jointly by researchers at State University of New York at Stony Brook and the University of Chicago, found that of all sexually active people, the people who reported being the most physically pleased and emotionally satisfied were married couples.[3]

One writer was rather straightforward, "Promoting marriage in America will mean for a lot more happy men and women." Sex in America reported that married sex beats all else. For example: "Married women had much higher rates of usually or always hav-ing orgasms, 75 percent, as compared to women who were never married and not cohabiting, 62 percent." And, the researchers wrote, "those having the most sex and enjoying it the most are the married people."[4]

Not only is sex better in marriage, it is best if you have had only one sexual partner in a lifetime. We now know "physical and emotional satisfaction start to decline when people have had more than one sexual partner."[5] God knows best about sex. God knows best about *marriage.*

MARRIAGE

Married people have healthier unions than couples who live together. Research from Washington State University revealed, "Cohabiting couples compared to married couples have less healthy relationships."[6]

Married people are generally better off in *all* measures of well-being. Researchers at UCLA explained that "cohabitors experienced significantly more difficulty in [subsequent] marriages with [issues of] adultery, alcohol, drugs and independence than couples who had not cohabited."[7] In fact, marriages preceded by cohabitation are fifty to one hundred percent *more* likely to break up than those marriages not preceded by cohabitation.[8]

"Wife beating" should more properly be called "girlfriend beating." According to the *Journal of Marriage and the Family,* "aggression is at least twice as common among cohabitors as it is among married partners."[9]

Married people enjoy better physical and mental health. Dr. Robert Coombs, a biobehavioral scientist at UCLA, conducted a review of more than 130 studies on the relationship between well-being and marital status, concluding that "there is an intimate link between the two." Married people have significantly lower rates of alcoholism, suicide, psychiatric care, and higher rates of self-reported happiness.[10]

Those in married relationships experience a lower rate of severe depression than people in any other category.[11] The annual rate of major depression per one hundred is as follows:

Married (never divorced)   1.5
Never married   2.4
Divorced once   4.1
Cohabiting   5.1
Divorced twice   5.8

The most careful recent study of the mental health of the married and unmarried looked at a nationwide sample of nearly thirteen thousand people. Married women were about thirty-three percent more likely than unmarried to rate their emotional health as "excellent." Unmarried women were more than twice as likely as married women to rate their emotional health as "poor."

Researchers at the University of Massachusetts say married people experience less disease, morbidity, and disability than do those who are divorced or separated. Their explanation: "One of the most consistent observations in health research is that the married enjoy better health than those of other [relational] statuses."[12] One study concerning men in particular revealed that nine out of ten men married at forty-eight will still be alive at sixty-five, while only six out of ten single men will be.

Men and women are at much greater risk of being assaulted if they are *not* married, reported the U.S. Department of Justice in

1994.[13] The rates per one thousand for general aggravated assaults against both males and females speak for themselves:

MALES
Married   5.5
Divorced or separated   13.6
Never married   23.4

FEMALES
Married   3.1
Divorced or separated   9.1
Never married   11.9

CHILDREN

The best environment to raise children is in a home with a father and a mother who are married to each other. On average, children do better in all areas when raised by two married parents who live together. One of the most authoritative works done in this area is by Dr. Sara McLanahan of Princeton University. In *Growing Up with a Single Parent,* she explains, "Children who grow up in a household with only one biological parent are worse off, on average, than children who grow up . . . with both of their biological parents, regardless of the parents' race or educational background."[14] Adolescents who have lived apart from one of their parents during some period of childhood are:

- Twice as likely to drop out of high school.
- Twice as likely to have a child before age twenty.
- One-and-a-half times as likely to be idle—out of school and out of work—in their late twenties.[15]

A study conducted at the University of Utah said that parental divorce hurts young children because it often leaves them in the care of highly stressed and irritable mothers.[16]

"Children without fathers more often have lowered academic performance, more cognitive and intellectual deficits, increased adjustment problems, and higher risks for psychosexual development problems."[17] Violent children are eleven times more likely not to live with their fathers and six times more likely to have parents who are not married.

Children not living with both biological parents are four times as likely to be suspended or expelled from school.[18] The *Heritage Foundation* noted in June 2000, "A million children a year see their parents divorce." Only forty-two percent of teens aged fourteen through eighteen live in a "first family," an intact, two-parent married family.

Children of divorce experience "anger, fear, sadness, worry, rejection, conflicting loyalties, lowered self-confidence, heightened anxiety, loneliness, more depressed moods, more suicidal thoughts," says the Heritage report, "The Effects of Divorce on America" by Dr. Patrick Fagan and Robert Rector. Compared to kids in intact homes, children of divorce face startling risks. They are twelve times more liable to be incarcerated as juveniles; fourteen times more prone to be physically abused by a single mother, and thirty-three times more at risk if she cohabits; three times more apt to get pregnant, and males commit suicide at sixfold higher rates.

The report also notes that many children of divorce become dysfunctional adults: "Even 30 years after the divorce, negative long-term effects were clearly present in the income, health and behavior of many of the grown offspring." They have more failed romantic relationships, a greater number of sexual partners, are two to three times as apt to cohabit, are less trusting of fiancées, less giving to them, and twice as likely to divorce. When both are from divorced homes, their risk of divorce is as much as 620 percent higher in early years of marriage. Thus the "marital instability of one generation is passed on to the next."[19]

Dr. David Popenoe, a noted family scholar from Rutgers University, explains that there can be no serious debate over this issue: "I know of few other bodies of data in which the weight of evidence is so decisively on one side of the issue. On the whole, for children, two-parent families are preferable. . . . If our prevailing views on family structure hinged solely on scholarly evidence, the current debate never would have arisen in the first place."[20]

Further, a sociologist at the University of Pennsylvania said, "Most studies show that children in stepfamilies do not do better than children in single-parent families; indeed, many indicate that, on average, children in remarriages do worse."[21] It is disturbing to note that stepfamilies are the second-fastest growing family structure in America. The fastest is created by out-of-wedlock births.[22]

Even the death of a parent is not as devastating to a child as losing one by divorce or desertion. Why? Single-parent families created by the death of a spouse have a natural protective mechanism distinguishing them from other single-parent families. Dr. James Egan, a child psychiatrist at Children's Hospital in Washington, D.C., provocatively asserts, "A dead father is a more effective father than a missing father."[23]

When a father (or mother) dies, he still maintains a place of authority, influence, and moral leadership in the home. Parents who have departed due to death usually leave positive reputations. Their pictures remain on the wall, they are talked about positively, and negative behavior on the part of a child can be corrected with a simple reminder: "Would your dad (or mom) approve of that kind of behavior?" If the father has abandoned the child or was never identified, the answer to that question is either "Who cares?" or even worse, "Who?"

In an article entitled "How Kids Mourn," *Newsweek* reported:

> The death of a parent can have devastating psychologi-
> cal consequences, including anxiety, depression, sleep
> disturbances, underachievement, and aggression. But
> so can a lot of other things, and losing a parent [by
> death] is actually less devastating than divorce. "We
> know that children tend to do better after a parental
> death than a divorce," says sociologist Andrew Cherlin
> of Johns Hopkins, "and that's a stunning statistic,
> because you'd think death would be harder."[24]

Actually there is nothing stunning about this at all. When a child, big or small, loses a parent by death, his mind reasons something like this: *If my daddy could be here, he would be here. But he's dead and so he can't.* On the other hand, if a child loses a parent by desertion or divorce, his mind reasons differently, thinking: *If my daddy wanted to be here, he would be here. I guess he doesn't want to be here, and it must be my fault.* This is the devastating fallout on children wounded by a divorce, a wound we now know often follows them into adulthood.[25]

And now that the 1990s are history and a new millennium has dawned, additional new research has come forth that makes the argument for marriage with even greater force. As noted earlier, in their blockbuster, *The Case for Marriage: Why Married People Are*

Happier, Healthier and Better Off Financially, authors Linda Waite, a professor of sociology at the University of Chicago, and Maggie Gallagher, director of the Marriage Project at the Institute for American Values in New York, reveal that married women living with their husbands are much less likely to be victims of domestic violence and even violence from strangers than are their single, separated, divorced, or cohabiting sisters.

> For most women, marriage is a safe haven. Marriage
> changes the relationship of the marriage partners for
> the good, giving them a stake in the well-being of each
> other and the family in a way other forms of "partner-
> ship" cannot. The public promise of marriage changes
> the way you think about yourself and your beloved; it
> changes the way you act and think about the future;
> and it changes how other people and other institutions
> treat you as well.[26]

An extensive survey of the data on marriage shows that married people, in general, are significantly healthier, both physically and mentally, than their nonmarried peers:

> They are far more affluent, even when living on only
> one income; women are safer, and men, even from
> backgrounds at "high-risk" for violence, are far less
> likely to commit crime; they report more satisfying
> sex lives than their single peers, even those who
> are cohabiting; and overall they are significantly hap-
> pier than folks in any other kind of relationship
> "arrangement."[27]

God knows best. The evidence is absolutely overwhelming and indisputable. He knows best about sex, marriage, and children. And yet we can still have doubts, worries, anxieties, and questions as we approach this divinely ordained institution. Fear can almost paralyze us. How can I know? How can I be sure this is the right person? Has the "case for marriage" received a positive verdict in my own heart? Let me encourage you to keep in mind four things as you attempt to settle this issue.

In my bed at night
I sought the one I love;
I sought him, but did not find him.
I will arise now and go about the city,
    through the streets and the plazas.
I will seek the one I love.
    I sought him, but did not find him. (vv. 1–2)

MARRIAGE IS THE RIGHT PLACE TO ENJOY SEXUAL PASSION (vv. 1–2)

A Barna Update[28] reported that "the goals that most adults identify as their top priorities in life are healthy living, possessing a high level of integrity, and keeping one marriage partner for life." These are good and admirable goals, things we hope, and maybe even dream, will come true.

Many Bible scholars believe this portion of Holy Scripture is a dream Shulammite had one night shortly before her marriage to Solomon. It was not a pleasant dream at first. In fact it was more like a nightmare. Still, in the midst of it we learn something of the passionate love she possessed for Solomon.

We also receive counsel concerning passion and its relationship to marriage.

SATISFY YOURSELF THIS IS THE RIGHT MATE (V. 1)

Shulammite's desire and passion for Solomon was an all-night affair, and it was intense. She was completely consumed with him in her thoughts. In her bed, where he would soon join her, she longed to have him now.

The themes of "seeking" and "finding" occur four times in these verses. The word translated "sought" or "looked" can also mean to desire, yearn, or long for. There is a feverishness in the word. There is passion. She was certain in her heart ("I sought the one I love"). He was the right man for her.

SAVE YOURSELF FOR THE RIGHT MOMENT (VV. 1–2)

She looked for or sought him, but she did not find him. She arose and, at night, went into and about the city, something dangerous and inappropriate for a young woman in the Middle East to do. So great was her desire for Solomon that she abandoned proper decorum and went in search for "the one I love." Still she did not find him. Why? The answer is simple: he's not there—yet!

She has saved herself for her wedding night. In so doing, she has honored both God and her husband. Sex, as we have noted, is God's good gift—and one to be enjoyed—but only in marriage. Hebrews 13:4 teaches that the marriage bed is undefiled. It is a place where God says to enjoy the pleasures of sexual passion and to do so fully.

Solomon is not there now in her bed or even at her side, but he will be soon. She has saved herself for the right moment. Understandably she wants that moment to be now, and she misses him. This is the passion God wants us to have for each other in marriage. Such passion is an indication that you have found the right person. Marriage is the right place to enjoy sexual passion.

The guards who go about the city found me.
  "Have you seen the one I
    love?" I asked them. (v. 3)

MARRIAGE IS THE RIGHT PLACE TO EXAMINE POTENTIAL PROBLEMS (V. 3)

In her dream Shulammite meets the guards of the city as she searches for Solomon. The significance of the guards in her dream is not all together clear. They could represent nothing important at all. On the other hand they could represent persons of authority and importance, persons of wisdom and counsel who could lend valuable assistance. These are men who "go about the city." They are wise in the ways of the street. They have observed the habits of humanity. They have seen things. They know.

They find her, and she questions them, "Have you seen the one I love?" Two lessons can be learned from this simple encounter.

PURSUE YOUR SPOUSE WITH HEALTHY ABANDONMENT

She again calls Solomon "the one I love." She is not ashamed for anyone, even strangers, to know how she feels. She loves him, and she is looking for him. She misses him and needs him. Her anxiety at his absence is normal and to be expected. As time goes on, after they are married, it will be a healthy sign in their relationship that they miss each other when they are apart but also that a security has developed in the relationship that puts fears and anxieties to rest.

That there would ever be a day they would enjoy being apart would be a telltale sign that their marriage was in serious trouble.

Charlotte and I knew a couple where the husband traveled a lot, often out of the country. I remember on one occasion seeing the wife and asking if her husband was away on business again, to which she said yes. I said, "It must be hard his being gone so much." To my surprise she said no. Actually, she enjoyed it when he was away. His absence allowed her to do what she wanted without worrying about him. Charlotte and I were not surprised that a short time later they separated, and eventually they divorced. Pursuing your spouse with a healthy abandonment is to be a lifelong adventure.

PURSUE YOUR SPOUSE WITH HELPFUL ADVICE

Shulammite's asking for help in finding Solomon again reminds us that asking questions, lots of questions, before marriage is wise and good. We should ask questions of others and of each other. It is impossible to know too much. We have already addressed an extensive number of questions couples should work through in preparing for marriage. Let's add a few more.

For many years now (more than fifty!), Dr. Howard Hendricks has taught at Dallas Theological Seminary. During that time he compiled a list he entitled "30 Questions Most Frequently Asked by Young Couples Looking Forward to Marriage." Let's look at these ourselves and see what young and inquiring minds want to know when marriage is on their mind.

Thirty Questions Most Frequently Asked by
Young Couples Looking Forward to Marriage
1. Where should a couple stop in petting before marriage?
2. Is jealousy part of love for your mate?

3. Who should control the purse strings?

4. When both are working, is the wife's money hers, or does it belong to both of them? If both work, who should support the family while (if) the husband continues his schooling?

5. Is there any reason the wife should not support the family while the husband continues his schooling?

6. Should the husband help with housework?

7. Should couples have a will drawn up soon after marriage?

8. Should a young couple carry insurance?

9. What are the effects of frequent business travel or unusual working hours on marital happiness?

10. To what extent should we discuss our pasts?

11. Is it true that people are not really "in love" until after they have been married for some years?

12. When we differ, how can we work out a happy adjustment?

13. Is it true that quarrels are never necessary?

14. If we come from divided families, can we profit by our parent's mistakes?

15. When we belong to two different churches, how do we work out our differences and what about children?

16. How can a couple keep in-laws in their place but still make them feel loved and necessary?

17. What should they do if he feels she does not give enough and she feels he does not give enough, they talk about it and still feel this way?

18. How soon after marriage should a couple plan to have children?

19. When considering having children, should the decision be primarily economic?

20. Are contraceptives safe to use? Do they lead to cancer or sterility?

21. What part does each partner have in the love play preceding and during intercourse?

22. Is every couple able to have satisfactory intercourse?

23. Is it harmful or wrong to have intercourse during a woman's menstruation?

24. Is there danger of constantly arousing sexual desires and not fulfilling this desire, in both male and female?

25. How does a woman know when she reaches a climax?

26. Do women undergo emotional changes during pregnancy and menstrual periods?

27. How important is it for couples to know their RH factor?

28. Are regular times for prayer important?

29. Are there occasions in marriage when divorce seems a reasonable and even proper solution?

30. If we find difficulties arising in our marriage, what immediate steps should we take?

I had just passed them
  when I found the one I love.
I held on to him and would not let him go
  until I brought him to my mother's house—
to the chamber of the one who conceived me. (v. 4)

MARRIAGE IS THE RIGHT PLACE TO EXPERIENCE NATURAL PROTECTION (V. 4)

Shulammite's persistence pays off as is often the case when it comes to romance. The guards leave, and suddenly there Solomon is, the one she loves. Notice two things she does that would let him know of her love and that we would do well to emulate.

HOLD ON TO HIM

"She held him and would not let him go." She had found her man, and she was not about to lose him again. She feels protected and secure in his presence, and I suspect he felt the same concerning her.

HONOR HIM

She took him back to her maternal home, a place that would also feel safe and secure. She is certain he is the man with whom she wishes to spend the rest of her life. There is no indication of resistance on Solomon's part. He loves her and desires her as much as she does him. He is honored by her attention and her intentions. This is indeed the woman for him as well. In sickness and in health, for better or for worse, till death do us part, they will be there for each other.

> *Young women of Jerusalem, I charge you,*
> > *by the gazelles and the wild does of the field:*
> *do not stir up or awaken love*
> > *until it is the appropriate time. (v. 5)*

MARRIAGE IS THE RIGHT PLACE TO EXERCISE SPIRITUAL PATIENCE (V. 5)

Marriage is as much about being the right person as finding the right person. When you are the right person, you can wait on God and trust both His plan and His timing. When you are the right person, you are ready for God to bring the other right person into your life.

For the second time in the Song (cf. 2:7) we hear the refrain calling us to patience, to wait. The refrain is in the form of an oath, a vow. Though the vow is made by the gazelles and the wild does, ultimately it is the Creator of these beautiful and active animals to whom Shulammite looks. What is her counsel? In a sense we come full circle back to verse 1.

MAKE A COMMITMENT TO GOD TO WAIT FOR THE RIGHT PERSON

We have received good counsel in how we can identify the right person. Be patient. Wait on the Lord. God always gives His best to those who leave the choices with Him.

MAKE A COMMITMENT TO GOD TO WAIT FOR THE RIGHT TIME

God's time is always the right time. When we wait and do marriage, sex, and romance on his schedule, we discover personally what we should have known all along: *God, indeed, knows best!*

I came across a story that provides a beautiful witness as we make the case for marriage. See if you don't agree.

Berry Mauve or Muted Wine?

He found me weeping bitterly in the hospital room. "What's wrong?" Richard asked, knowing we both had reason to cry. In the past 48 hours, I had discovered the lump in my breast was cancerous; the cancer had spread to my lymph nodes; and there was a possible spot on my brain.

I was 32 years old and the mother of three beautiful children. Richard pulled me tight and tried to

comfort me. Many had expressed amazement at the
peace that had overwhelmed me from the beginning.
God was my comfort the moment before I found out
I had cancer, and He remained the same after. But it
seemed to Richard that all that had crashed in the few
moments he had been out of the room.

He held me tight. "It's all been too much, hasn't it,
Suz?" he said. "That's not it," I cried and held up the
hand mirror I had found in the drawer. Richard was
puzzled. "I didn't know it was like this," I cried. I had
found the mirror in the nightstand and was shocked at
my reflection. I didn't even recognize myself. After the
surgery, I groaned in my sleep and well-meaning
friends had freely pushed the self-dispensing medica-
tion to ease what they thought was pain. Unfortunately
I was allergic to morphine and had swelled like a
sausage. Betadine from the surgery stained my neck,
shoulder and chest and it was too soon for a bath.

A tube hung out of my side draining the fluid from
the surgical site. My left shoulder and chest was
wrapped tightly in gauze where I had lost a portion of
my breast. My long, curly hair was matted into one big
wad.

What hit me the hardest was that over 100 people
had come to see me over the past 48 hours and they
had all seen this brown and white, swollen, makeup-
less, matted-haired, gray-gowned woman that used to
be me. Where had I gone?

Richard left the room. Within moments he came
back, his arms laden with small bottles. He pulled

pillows out of the closet and dragged a chair over to
the sink. He unraveled my IV and tucked the long tube
from my side in his shirt pocket. He reached down and
picked me up and scooted the IV stand with one foot
as he carried me over to the chair. As he sat me down
gently on his lap, he cradled my head in his arms over
the sink and began to run warm water through my
hair. He poured the small bottles he had confiscated
from the cart in the hall over my hair and washed and
conditioned my long curls. He wrapped my hair in a
towel and he carried me, the tube, and IV stand back
over to the bed. All of this done so gently that not one
stitch was disturbed.

My husband, who has never blow-dried his thick
dark hair in his life, took out the blow drier and dried
my hair, the whole while entertaining me as he pre-
tended to give beauty tips. He then proceeded, with the
experience of watching me for the past 12 years, to fix
my hair. I laughed as he bit his lip, more serious than
any beauty school student. He bathed my shoulder and
neck with a warm washcloth, careful to not disturb the
area around the surgery and rubbed lotion into my
skin. Then he opened my makeup bag and began to
apply makeup. I will never forget the laughter we
shared as he tried to apply my mascara and blush.
I opened my eyes wide and held my breath as his
hands shook as he brushed the mascara on my lashes.
He rubbed my cheeks with tissue to blend in the blush.

With the last touch, he held up two lipsticks.
"Which one? Berry mauve or muted wine?" he asked.

He applied the lipstick like an artist painting on a can-
vas and then held the little mirror in front of me. I was
human again. A little swollen, but I smelled clean, my
hair hung softly over my shoulders and I recognized
who I was. "What do you think?" he asked. I began to
cry again, this time because I was grateful. "No, baby.
You'll mess up my makeup job," he said and then
I burst into laughter.

   During that difficult time in our lives, I was given
only a 10–40% chance of survival over five years. That
was nine years ago. I made it through those years with
laughter, with God's comfort, and with the help of a
man brought into my life named Richard. We will celebrate our 21st anniversary this year with our three children—our twins, who are 17, and our 18 year old
daughter. Richard understood what others might have
taken for vanity in the midst of tragedy. Everything
I had ever taken for granted had been shaken in those
hours—the fact that I would watch my children grow,
my health, my future. With one small act of kindness,
Richard gave me normalcy. I will always see that
moment as one of the kindest gestures of our
marriage.[29]

The case for marriage is made. The evidence is irrefutable.
Now you be the judge.

Chapter 7

How to Have a Great Wedding

THE SONG OF SONGS 3:6–11

Weddings and marriage for life are out! Cohabitation, trial runs, and prenups are in. At least this is the picture you get if you listen to the prophets of popular culture.

> *Monica Schmidt:* "It's just a piece of paper to me. I consider myself married without that . . . There's more freedom, I'm allowed to do whatever I like."

> *John Nielsen:* "It's outmoded. I'm just as committed to the relationship as I would be if I were married." Claiming to be emotionally abused from his parents' divorce and now in therapy John adds, "Anything that comes before my recovery has to go. If I'm not putting myself first, the children are not going to see someone who is looking after themselves."

> *Robin Hill,* in a cohabiting arrangement: "I've got a life too. If I thought 'Oh, this isn't doing anything for me,' I'd move on." When asked about a wedding and

marriage she joked, "I thought 'well, we do need a new toaster!' but I can't see the need to be married."[1]

Aline Fesquet and Frank Embert who entered into a "civil solidarity pact" in France: "For us, it is a step forward in our relationship, but without the family and all the baggage."[2]

The numbers would certainly indicate that cohabiting is the rage of the day. The number of cohabiting couples has risen from 439,000 in 1960 to 4.2 million in 1998.[3] With so many adopting this new lifestyle, it must be producing some really good results, right? Wrong. Consider the following data:

1. Only about one-sixth of live-ins last at least three years, and only one-tenth endure five years or more.[4]
2. Living together before marriage increases the risk of divorce. One study found an increased risk of forty-six percent. Living together outside marriage increases the risk of domestic violence for women and the risk of physical and sexual abuse for children. One study found that the risk of domestic violence for women in cohabiting relationships was double that in married relationships; the risk is even greater for child abuse. Unmarried couples have lower levels of happiness and well-being than married couples.[5]
3. Couples who live together first are more likely to have an affair during marriage than those who don't.[6]
4. Cohabiting couples are three times more likely to say "hitting, shoving and throwing things" occurred between them

and their partner the previous year.[7] Pamela Smock summarizes the situation well: "While common sense suggests that premarital cohabitation should offer couples an opportunity to learn about each other, increasing their chances for a successful marriage, the evidence suggests just the opposite. Premarital cohabitation tends to be associated with lower marital quality and increased risk of divorce."[8]

So what is the problem? Rita DeMaria, I think, hits the nail on the head when she says, "Being single is a choice that most people do not choose. People want to be married." However, "some people have never seen a good marriage."[9] For far too many, their perspective on marriage can be easily summed up. First comes the engagement ring, then comes the wedding ring, and then comes the suffering. Perhaps the "case against marriage" is really not too hard to understand, given what some people have seen and experienced. This radical skepticism toward God's divine plan was pointedly addressed by Larissa Phillips in an article entitled "The Case Against Matrimony: If Marriage is Risky, Doomed and Expensive, Why Bother?" It is lengthy, but the message is worth hearing. She writes:

> Nov. 18, 1999. The National Marriage Project at
> Rutgers University recently announced the findings of
> a new study: the marriage rate has dropped 43 percent
> since 1960, and increasing numbers of young people
> are choosing to stay unmarried. The U.S. Census
> Bureau came out with related big news last week: The
> number of babies born to unwed parents has
> increased fivefold since the 1930s, owing, for the most
> part, to more and more couples rejecting marriage,
> even after the birth of a child. Suddenly everyone is

scrambling to understand. Well, I get it, and I didn't
have to scramble to understand. In fact, what interests
me is not why the members of my generation (X, if
you will) are getting married less, but why anyone is
surprised.

What did everyone—i.e., the baby boomers—expect?
As the unmarried mother of a new baby, I am the
object of much indignant scrutiny among the older
generations, who seem to have conveniently forgotten
the past 30 years, in which almost everyone I know has
been emotionally pummeled in some way by divorce.
As my boyfriend asked at a recent family gathering,
while playing a board game in which you have to
prompt the other players to supply a particular word:
"What must you do before you get married?" The
answer, of course: get divorced. My father and his wife
thought this was hilarious. And yet aging boomers seem
shocked and befuddled that someone would choose to
avoid the whole swampy mess of broken vows and
failed traditions that they've left in their wake.

People over 40 flinched with disdain when I first
announced my pregnancy. "Oh," they would exclaim,
barely masking their disapproval. "And . . . what do your
parents think?" They struggled to understand my lack
of panic. "Are you going to keep it?" they asked, wide-
eyed. As if the '60s, '70s and '80s never happened. As if
at least one-third of marriages don't fail. As if everyone
in my family and my boyfriend's family, grandparents
included, hadn't broken their marriage vows. At least
once. "What's with all these people in our family

having babies without getting married?" my middle-aged uncle (who is divorced and recently broke up with his live-in girlfriend) asked my 40-ish aunt (who recently divorced her husband because he'd taken up with a married woman, who is now his third wife; my aunt is now living with her boyfriend).

The worst is from my parents. "Marriage is very important," my mother said. "It establishes a bond that you just can't get otherwise." I wanted to argue with her, but she was getting ready to leave the country with her new husband. They spend their summers at their cottage up in Nova Scotia, a good 20-hour trip away from the rest of us. "Studies show that married couples are better off financially than single people," my father's youngish second wife insisted. It's probably true that she is better off financially since marrying my father, but I wasn't sure how that applied to me. When my boyfriend and I looked into getting married, we found out that we would pay an extra $2,000 each year in taxes.

If marriage is risky, doomed and expensive, well, why bother? "You just should," my father offered in that magnanimous, ain't-life-grand manner he developed shortly after re-entering the singles scene when I was a teenager. My father is big on the "shoulds" of life, with some reason. He has always done everything he was supposed to, even as a divorced father; he never even bad-mouthed my mom (nor did she ever trash him, for that matter). But the fact that my parents divorced well—and they really did—doesn't grant them immunity from their actions. The fact that my

uncles and aunts and grandparents and family friends
felt they had absolutely no choice other than to divorce
doesn't change the outcome. They still got divorced, all
of them. They still showed my generation, by example
and by forcing us to go along with their example, that
marriage was something easily and amicably exited
from. Marriage, they said, was not that big of a deal.
Premarital sex is fine. (Or at least that's what they
implied when they presented their boyfriends and girlfriends at the breakfast table—before we were even out
of high school.) Families, they said, do not need to stay
together if things become too boring.

I would have more sympathy for divorced people if
their lives had improved by getting out of terrible marriages that (apparently) couldn't be survived for another
moment. But the ones I'm familiar with continue to
associate with flawed human beings. These second and
third marriages still seem to require work, and still have
shortcomings. My mother and father, for example, still
struggle with the same issues that plagued their marriage to each other. The only difference is, older and
wiser, they both seem more willing to compromise, to
sacrifice and to accept. I am not whining about or
regretting the events of the last three decades. When my
parents divorced in the late '70s, we children went along
with it like troupers. When they started bringing home
boyfriends and girlfriends in the '80s, we ultimately
accepted these new people into our family. Sometimes,
the new people went away. And we dealt with the
divorces and separations all over again. And accepted

the new people all over again. Fine. Exhausting, but fine.
It's a wonder we 18- to 35-year-olds even have the
energy to date. (And maybe some of us don't.) But for
myself, the scattered, patchwork concept of family
I grew up with has only increased my quest for commitment. I've seen firsthand the pain and futility of divorce
culture and I don't intend to relive it, or to drag my children through the nightmare of watching their parents
flirt with strangers. My decision not to marry does not
indicate a desire for a life of debauchery and half-
formed commitments. Quite the opposite . . . but we
have no fantasies about coasting through the next 50
years on the coattails of a weakened and disparaged contract that, thanks to boomer innovation, now includes
options like pre-nup clauses. Considering everything
we've seen, bearing the weight of our relationship on
our own backs seems a hell of a lot wiser than leaning
on the white-laced and satin-cummerbunded follies of
our parents. Thanks, but we're looking for more than
just a party, a round of toasts and a validity stamp from
Uncle Sam to get us to that golden anniversary. Our parents, on the other hand, seem to believe in marriage
more than they do in monogamy. Like I said, that's fine.
Every generation has its torch to carry. But when this
particular generation, which grooved to its own beat
and stomped on every tradition that seemed too square,
too inhibiting or just plain boring, turns around with
nostalgia in its eyes and questions my choices, I have to
protest. My generation would just as soon steer clear of
the fatuous, feel-good mess of getting divorced and

remarried. The tradition that was passed down to us—
in which divorce is a logical and expected conclusion to
a marriage—is one we would just as soon pass by. . . . Of
course marriage is on the decline. But don't blame us.
The boomers started it.[10]

We could easily get depressed from all of this, until we realize
that there is a common thread that runs through all the stories we
have heard. It could be put in the form of a simple question:
Where is God in all of this? He doesn't even get honorable mention. Marriage, after all, was His idea. He has a pattern. He has a
plan. Marriage can be different when we invite the Holy Trinity to
honor the wedding and direct the marriage. Our expectations,
hopes, and dreams can and will be radically altered and trans-
formed, and all for the better.

I want to focus particularly on what begins a marriage: the
wedding. This is what is described in Song of Songs 3:6–11. It is a
fantastic and beautiful scene. What are the distinctive characteristics and elements of the wedding God has planned for each one of
us? God's Word addresses four things in this text.

> *Who is this coming up from the wilderness*
>   *like columns of smoke,*
> *scented with myrrh and frankincense*
>   *from every fragrant powder of the merchant? (v. 6)*

A GREAT WEDDING WILL BE A PUBLIC CELEBRATION
(V. 6)

A wedding should be one of the most exciting and important
days in any person's life. It should not be entered into lightly or

without careful consideration. God's plan is that you experience it only once until death parts you and your spouse. It legitimately should be a time of joy and laughter, happiness and hope. Solomon notes two particular facets which should accompany the public celebration.

A WEDDING IS A TIME THAT SHOULD BE SPECIAL

Marriages in the ancient Near East were civil rather than religious affairs. Most often they took place in a home. A central aspect of the wedding ceremony was a procession to the bride's home led by the groom. He would go and gather her unto himself, and then escort her back to their new home where the actual wedding ceremony would take place. The wedding feast sometimes would last up to a week. The marriage, however, would be consummated on the first night. The marriage was a special ritual in which the man publicly pledged himself to his bride and she to him. Solomon and his entourage have come to Shulammite's home to get her. The pageantry and procession would honor Shulammite and appropriately sanctify the day in all of its significance. The wedding day is not just another day. It is a once in a lifetime event. It is indeed special.

A WEDDING IS A TIME TO MAKE A STATEMENT

Solomon wants the world to know how much he loves this woman. As Shulammite comes out of the wilderness and into the city, "columns of smoke" appear to accompany her. We learn, however, that it is actually "myrrh and frankincense" mingled with "every fragrant powder of the merchant." The burning of these spices would appeal to both the senses of sight and smell.

These spices also would have been costly. This day would be the beginning of their new life together. Their commitment to each other is strong and secure. The celebration—and even the extravagance—of the procession is appropriate for such an important occasion. They intend to make a statement.

Without being opulent and ostentatious, a wedding should be a celebration. It should be festive but also spiritual. It should be a public testimony of the value we place on our mate and the worth of companionship. It is not God's plan that it take place quietly behind closed doors. It is a public affair!

> *Look! Solomon's royal litter*
> *surrounded by 60 warriors*
> *from the mighty of Israel.*
> *All of them are skilled with swords*
> *and trained in warfare.*
> *Each has his sword at his side*
> *to guard against the terror of the night. (vv. 7–8)*

A Great Wedding Contains a Promise of Protection (vv. 7–8)

When Solomon came for Shulammite, he did not come alone. He brought his companions. He brought his best. An escort of striking presence accompanied him. They enabled Solomon to make two statements about the marriage he and his bride would enjoy.

Marriage Provides Safety (v. 7)

The "60 warriors," valiant men "from the mighty of Israel" were friends of the groom. They were Solomon's closest and most trusted confidants. Most likely they were his royal bodyguard, whose duty it was to protect the king and his family. By their presence they served as a pledge of safety from Solomon to Shulammite. They are warriors of "Israel," of the nation.[11] They surround Solomon's "royal litter" or carriage. She is safe under his protective care and concern. He will spare nothing to assure her heart and mind that she will be well cared for.

MARRIAGE PROVIDES SECURITY (V. 8)

The "60 warriors from the mighty of Israel" are experienced and skilled. Shulammite can put to rest any fears that might trouble her heart. They have their weapons and are experienced in the affairs of battle. Even at night when evil and wicked persons are especially active to do their shameful deeds, she can be at peace that all is safe and secure. Her man will see to it. He will be her champion and defender.

This marriage is no shaky situation with nagging doubts and unanswered questions. Shulammite is not marrying some cad who will abuse her. She is marrying a real man who will love and protect her.

Tommy Nelson provides a helpful word at this point in the context of the wedding ceremony. He writes:

> Part of the safety and security of the wedding ceremony will be evident in the people who serve as your best man, maid or matron of honor, groomsmen, and bridesmaids. Choose godly people who will support you fully in the vows you make. As a whole, those who witness your marriage should be like a holy hedge of protection around you, keeping you focused toward

each other inside the circle of matrimony, and keeping
out anybody who might try to destroy your marriage.
Don't ask someone to stand up for you who isn't completely committed to you, to your marriage, and in
general, to the sanctity and value of marriage. Such a
person will not encourage you to work through problems in your marriage. Such a person will not do the
utmost to help you and your spouse when you need
help. And they may embarrass you at rehearsal dinner![12]

King Solomon made a sedan chair for himself
*   with wood from Lebanon.*
He made its posts of silver,
*   its back of gold,*
*   and its seat of purple.*
Its interior is inlaid with love
*   by the young women of Jerusalem. (vv. 9–10)*

A GREAT WEDDING INCLUDES A PLEDGE
OF COMMITMENT (VV. 9–10)

The missing word in cohabiting relationships is the "c" word:
commitment. When a man and woman come together to say the
"I do's," commitment envelopes each and every vow. There is a
pledge of physical, spiritual, emotional, and personal commitment. In particular, two things are said.

ALL THAT I HAVE BELONGS TO YOU (VV. 9–10)

The carriage in which Solomon brought Shulammite to their
wedding was fine! It was made of the best materials money could

buy. The wood was from Lebanon. The timbers from these forests were in great demand throughout the ancient Near East.[13] It was from this wood that Solomon had carved his "sedan chair" or carriage. Added to this were "posts of silver;" a "back of gold," and a "seat of purple." All of this was exquisitely beautiful and expensive. It was Solomon's way of saying, "I will keep nothing back from you. All I have now belongs to you. You will always get my best."

Today, sometimes even in marriage, all that we have is not shared with our mate. In 1999, I was sad to learn that the best-selling book in Amazon.com's marriage category was *How to Write Your Own Premarital Agreement*. A publicist at Source books, where they hang the congratulatory plaque, said, "Kind of funny, isn't it? We put out all these books on love and marriage, and this is the bestseller."[14] A wedding that honors God and our mate does not come with strings attached or things held back. If you are not confident that your potential mate is worthy of all that belongs to you, perhaps you should reconsider your potential mate and why you are even thinking about marrying this person in the first place.

ALL MY LOVE BELONGS TO YOU (V. 10)

The interior of Solomon's carriage was unusual. It was "inlaid with love by the young women of Jerusalem." Some students of the Bible believe mosaics depicting love adorned the interior of the carriage. Duane Garrett suggests "inlaid with love" alludes to an association between "sedan chair" and "bed" and is a subtle hint at their approaching wedding night.[15] Whatever is true of the particular details, the main point is clear: they loved each other, and they pledged that love to each other at their wedding.

Sometime back I came across an article in a popular fashion magazine that contrasted *love* with *lust*. If we would be honest, in the red-hot passions that lead to marriage, we are not always sure of or even in control of our mind, will, and emotions. We have reached hormone heaven. Who needs to think at a time like this? Answer: All of us! All of us need to weigh carefully what is going on and to make sure that what we have is lasting love and not passing lust. Love does not equal sex, and sex does not equal love. Note the stark contrast that exists between love and lust. Give to each category strong consideration as it relates to your potential mate and partner for life.

Love

1. **Focuses on the other**

    "Let each of you look not only for his own interests, but also for the interests of others" (Philippians 2:4 NKJV).

2. **Leads to fulfillment**

    "To know the love of Christ which passes knowledge; that you may be filled with all the fullness of God . . . who is able to do exceedingly abundantly above all that we ask or think, according to the power that works in us" (Ephesians 3:19, 20 NKJV).

3. **Brings satisfaction**

    "No discipline seems pleasant . . . but later it produces a harvest of righteousness and peace for those who have been trained by it" (Hebrews 12:11 NIV).

4. **Encourages self-control**

    "I discipline my body and bring it into subjection" (I Corinthians 9:27 NKJV).

5. **Desires to live by the Spirit**

   "Live by the Spirit, and you will not gratify the desires of the sinful nature" (Galatians 5:16 NIV).

6. **Includes Christ**

   "Clothe yourselves with the Lord Jesus Christ, and do not think about how to gratify the desires of the sinful nature" (Romans 13:14 NIV).

7. **Seeks God to gain its desires**

   "Delight yourself in the Lord and He will give you the desires of your heart" (Psalm 37:4 NIV).

8. **Prevents sin**

   "Love your neighbor as yourself. But if you bite and devour one another, take heed that you are not consumed by one another" (Galatians 5:14, 15 NKJV).

9. **Nourishes the soul**

   "May God Himself, the God of peace, sanctify you through and through. May your whole spirit, soul and body be kept blameless" (I Thessalonians 5:23 NIV).

10. **Commits to one another ("free love" is a contradiction of terms)**

    "You have been called to liberty; only do not use liberty as an opportunity for the flesh, but by love serve one another" (Galatians 5:13 NKJV).

Lust

1. **Focuses on self**

   "You have been called to liberty; only do not use liberty as an opportunity for the flesh" (Galatians 5:13 NKJV).

2. **Leads to frustration**

   "You want something, but don't get it. You kill and covet, but you cannot have what you want" (James 4:2 NIV).

3. **Continually wants more**

   "They are separated from the life of God . . . and have given themselves over to sensuality so as to indulge in every kind of impurity, with a continual lust for more" (Ephesians 4:18–19 NIV).

4. **Enslaves self**

   "To whom you present yourselves servants to obey, you are that one's servants . . . you have presented your members as servants to uncleanness, and lawlessness" (Romans 6:16, 19 NKJV).

5. **Desires to gratify the sinful nature with things contrary to the Spirit**

   "The sinful nature desires what is contrary to the Spirit" (Galatians 5:17 NIV). *"The acts of the sinful nature are obvious: sexual immorality, impurity and debauchery; idolatry and witchcraft; hatred, discord, jealousy, fits of rage, selfish ambition, dissensions, factions and envy; drunkenness, orgies and the like"* (Galatians 5:19–21 NIV).

6. Excludes Christ

"Since they did not think it worthwhile to retain the knowledge of God, He gave them over to a depraved mind … they have become filled with every kind of wickedness, evil, greed and depravity" (Romans 1:28, 29 NIV).

7. Sins to gratify its desires

"All of us also lived among them at one time, gratifying the cravings of our sinful nature and following its desires and thoughts" (Ephesians 2:3 NIV).

8. Entices with evil desires

"But each one is tempted when, by his own evil desire, he is dragged away and enticed" (James 1:14 NIV).

9. Wars against the soul

"I urge you, as aliens and strangers in the world, to abstain from sinful desires, which war against your soul" (1 Peter 2:11 NIV).

10. Avoids commitment and leads to tragedy

"Don't lust for their beauty. Don't let their coyness seduce you. For a prostitute will bring a man to poverty, and an adulteress may cost him his very life" (Proverbs 6:25, 26 TLD).[16]

Come out, young women of Zion,
*   and gaze at King Solomon,*
*   wearing the crown his mother placed on him*
*   the day of his wedding—*
*   the day of his heart's rejoicing. (v. 11)*

A WEDDING HAS THE APPROVAL OF OTHERS (V. 11)

Sociologist Barbara Dafoe Whitehead has said, "Courtship is dying, lasting marriage is in crisis . . . kiss marriage goodbye. . . . Today it's hookup, breakup and get even. Is everybody happy?"[17] Newspaper columnist Suzanne Fields says in today's world women are not winning but losing, and losing big time. She directs our attention to the self-help section of our bookstores for a quick perusal of titles: *The Heartbreak Handbook; Getting Over Him; How to Heal the Hurt by Hating; Dumped: A Survival Guide for the Woman Who's Been Left by the Man;* and my personal favorite: *The Woman's Book of Revenge: Getting Even When "Mr. Right" Turns Out to Be All Wrong.*

Sometimes Mr. Right turns out to be Mr. Wrong. Cinderella turns out to be a wicked witch. Is there one last word of counsel that Solomon might give us to guide us away from such a disaster? Yes there is, and it is simply this: Make sure you have the approval and blessing of others. There is wisdom in the counsel of many.

OUR FRIENDS WILL APPROVE

Notice that "the young women of Zion" come out to join in the celebration of the wedding. They approve. They are enthusiastic. In their mind this is a good and wonderful thing that is about to happen. They like Solomon when he is with Shulammite. She brings out the best in him, not the worst, when they are together. The same is true for Shulammite. She is a better and more beautiful woman when she is with Solomon. That is a good sign for which we should be on the lookout. My mate makes me better and others notice.

OUR FAMILIES WILL APPROVE

Solomon's mother approved of Shulammite. The potential for in-law problems does not loom over the wedding, as is too often the case. She had prepared for him a crown similar to an Olympian laurel wreath, which symbolized the gladness and joy of his wedding day. According to Rabbinic tradition, crowns were worn by the bridegroom and the bride until the destruction of Jerusalem in A.D. 70.[18] This was a day of happiness not only for the king and his queen but for all who shared in this wonderful event. Those who loved Solomon and Shulammite most were confident this marriage was meant to be and meant to last. Their approval is no guarantee, but it is an indication of the confidence both family and friends had in the rightness of this union. This is something every wise couple will carefully consider as they work to have a great wedding and a great marriage.

On April 13, 2000, an unusual thing occurred on the campus of a Baptist seminary in Wake Forest, North Carolina. Approximately 550 couples, hand in hand and heart to heart, reaffirmed their marriage vows in a worship service and signed a covenant pledging to "exalt the sacred nature and permanence of the marriage covenant." The vows, penned by Paige Patterson and his wife, Dorothy, beautifully mirror the language of Ephesians 5:21–33 and are a wonderful expression of the covenantal commitment a husband and wife should pledge to each other on the day of their wedding. They also express the devotion and commitment that should characterize a marriage until death separates.

Husbands
My precious and honored wife, this day I renew
before God my covenant with you. I covenant today,

sacrificially to love you as Jesus loves His church.
I covenant to bestow always upon you abundant
honor. I will seek to know your needs and to provide
for them materially, physically, mentally, and emotionally. I will seek your well-being, happiness and
success above my own. Above all, I covenant to be the
spiritual leader of our union, to provide a spiritual
example through my walk with Christ, to teach the
Bible, to pray for my family, and to lead family worship. I will be faithful to you physically, mentally, and
emotionally and avoid all that is pornographic,
impure, or unholy. I will not be angry or bitter
against you nor allow the sun to go down on my
wrath. I will not keep books on evil. I will cultivate
tender affection for you both in private and in public.
I will compassionately give to you my body and
spirit in the union which we alone enjoy together.
I covenant this day to accept the role of servant
leader, and to be to my children and grandchildren,
should God grant, a compassionate, encouraging, and
guiding father. This day, I seal this covenant for as
long as we both shall live.

Wives
My precious and honored husband, this day I renew
before God my covenant with you. I covenant this day
to love and respect you with all the fervency of my
being. I covenant to make our home a place of repose
and comfort. I will honor you as the spiritual leader of
our home. I will devote myself to you and the offspring

God may give above all others. I will graciously submit
to your servant leadership never allowing the sun to go
down on my wrath. I will not keep books on evil. I will
regard my responsibilities as wife and mother as priority above all else except God. I will seek your well-
being, happiness, and success rather than my own.
I will compassionately give to you my body and spirit
in the union which we alone enjoy together. This day,
I seal this covenant for as long as we both shall live.[19]

Chapter 8

The Beauty and Blessings of Sex as God Planned It

THE SONG OF SONGS 4:1–5:1

In an article entitled, "What They Didn't Teach You About Sex in Sunday School," Peggy Fletcher Stack writes, "Many people assume the Bible has just one message about sex: Don't do it."[1] Anyone who says that obviously has not read the Bible. God, in His Word, has a lot to say about sex, and much of it is good.

Sex as God designed it is good, exciting, intoxicating, powerful, and unifying. Though the Bible is not a book on sex, it does contain a complete theology of sexuality: the purposes for sex, warnings against its misuse, and a beautiful picture of ideal physical intimacy as set forth in the Song of Songs. The one-flesh relationship (cf. Gen. 2:24) is the most intense physical intimacy and the deepest spiritual unity possible between a husband and wife. God always approves of this relationship in which husband and wife meet each other's physical needs in sexual intercourse (cf. Prov. 5:15–21).

Paul indicates that sexual adjustment in marriage can affect the Christian life, especially prayer (cf. 1 Cor. 7:5). Both husband

and wife have definite and equal sexual needs which are to be met in marriage (1 Cor. 7:3), and each is to meet the needs of the other and not his own (Phil. 2:3–5). God gave us the good gift of sex for several important reasons. These purposes include: (1) knowledge (cf. Gen. 4:1), (2) intimate oneness (Gen. 2:24), (3) comfort (Gen. 24:67), (4) the creation of life (Gen. 1:28), (5) play and pleasure (Song 2:8–17; 4:1–16), and (6) avoiding temptation (1 Cor. 7:2–5).

A husband is commanded to find satisfaction (Prov. 5:19) and joy (Eccles. 9:9) in his wife and to concern himself with meeting her unique needs (Deut. 24:5; 1 Pet. 3:7). A wife also has responsibilities. These include: (1) availability (1 Cor. 7:3–5), (2) preparation and planning (Song 4:9ff.), (3) interest (Song 4:16; 5:2), and (4) sensitivity to unique masculine needs (Gen. 24:67). The feeling of oneness experienced by husband and wife in the physical, sexual union should remind both partners of the even more remarkable oneness that the spirit of a man and a woman experiences with God in spiritual new birth (John 3).

There is beauty and blessing in the Christian bedroom. Here God says eat and drink deeply (5:1)! We have arrived (finally!) at the wedding night. The bride and groom are alone with only God as the unseen but welcomed guest. Here before us the couple consummates their marriage in intimate sexual union. Our passage, in exquisite poetry, provides for us a portrait of what a Christian bedroom should be.

> *How beautiful you are, my darling.*
> *How very beautiful!*
> *Behind your veil,*
> > *your eyes are doves.*

Your hair is like a flock a goats
    streaming down Mt. Gilead.
Your teeth are like a flock of newly shorn sheep
    coming up from the washing,
each one having a twin,
    and not one missing.
Your lips are like a scarlet cord,
    and your mouth is lovely.
Behind your veil,
    your brow is like a slice of pomegranate.
Your neck is like the tower of David,
    constructed in layers.
A thousand bucklers are hung on it—
    all of them shields of warriors.
Your breasts are like two fawns,
    twins of a gazelle, that feed among the lilies.
Before the day breaks
    and the shadows flee,
I'll make my way to the mountain of myrrh
    and the hill of frankincense.
You are absolutely beautiful, my darling,
    with no imperfection in you. (vv. 1–7)

LET IT BE A PLACE OF SATISFYING ATTRACTIVENESS (VV. 1–7)

These verses are a song of admiration from the groom to his bride. The time for the sexual consummation of their marriage has arrived, and yet it will not happen until verse 16. True romance is "an environment of affection" in which sexual union will occur more often and with greater satisfaction. In other words, some essential preliminaries must precede the main event. Unfortunately, this is not always clear to a male. Having been aroused sexually, he is now on the prowl as a predator, and his bride can certainly feel the part of prey. Solomon was sensitive to this, and so he begins with the most important sex organ we have: the mind! Thinking about how his new wife might feel, he chooses first to cultivate an atmosphere of acceptance through carefully chosen words.

MEN: MEET YOUR WIFE'S NEED FOR VERBAL SUPPORT (vv. 1–7)

Three times, both at the beginning and the end of this song, Solomon tells Shulammite she is "beautiful." Twice he calls her his "darling." In verse 7 he says there is "no imperfection in you." In his eyes she is the perfect woman for him.

Women are verbal creatures. They are moved by what they hear and by what they feel. "To a great extent, she thinks and feels [about herself] the way a man leads her to think and feel."[2] A man must learn to touch her heart (her mind) through her ear. This helps her feel good about herself, and it relaxes, prepares, and motivates her to give herself in passionate lovemaking to her husband. A wise man will understand the value of words, the right words, in preparation for sexual intimacy.

A study in *Psychology Today* noted that women are more likely to be disappointed with marriage than men, especially in the context of romance. Why?

> One explanation is that as compared with men, they
> have higher expectations for intimacy, and thus react

more negatively to conjugal reality. In a major
national survey conducted in 1976 by the Institute for
Social Research at the University of Michigan, more
wives than husbands said that they wished their
spouse talked more about thoughts and feelings, and
more wives felt resentment and irritation with husbands than vice versa. The researchers conclude: In
marriage . . . women talk and want verbal responsiveness of the kind they have had with other women, but
their men are often silent partners, unable to respond
in kind.[3]

WOMEN: MEET YOUR HUSBAND'S NEED FOR VISUAL STIMULATION (VV. 1–6)

If a woman is a creature of the ear, a man is a creature of the
eye. He is moved by what he sees. Verses 1–6 are a continuation of
Solomon's song of admiration as he praises eight different parts of
his wife's body. This would continue to meet her need for verbal
support, especially as we unlock the doors to the Ancient Near
Eastern images we encounter. At the same time these verses also
teach us something about the male and how visual he is when it
comes to sex. A brief survey of these verses makes clear that
Shulammite was not clothed in sweats, flannel, or burlap!
Apparently, only a veil covered her eyes. The rest of her body was
in full view; and Solomon liked, he loved, what he saw. Still his
patience and understanding are singularly remarkable. What an
incredible example he sets for men everywhere.

Women in the Ancient Near East wore a veil only on special
occasions such as the day of their wedding. Solomon says, "Behind
your veil, your eyes are doves." The veil both hides and enhances

her beauty. His likening of her eyes to doves conveys ideas of peace and purity, tranquility and tenderness, gentleness and innocence (cf. 1:15; 2:14; 5:2). Her eyes speak; they communicate to her husband that she has been calmed and set at rest by his kind and affirming words.

"Your hair is like a flock of goats streaming down Mount Gilead" would probably not get a guy very far in our day, but it would have been lovely music to the ears of Shulammite. Viewed from afar, a herd of black goats streaming or skipping down a mountainside as the sun glistened on their black hair was a beautiful sight. As Shulammite prepared to give herself to her husband, she let her hair down. Cascading down her neck and across her shoulders, her beautiful wavy locks entice the sexual desires of Solomon. Mount Gilead was a mountain range east of the Jordan River and northeast of the Dead Sea. It was known for its good and fertile pastures. Shulammite is herself vigorous and fertile on this their wedding night. Letting her hair down signals to Solomon her readiness for him.

Verses 2–3 focus on the beauty of her mouth. Her teeth are clean, bright, and white; none are missing! Her "lips are like a scarlet cord" (thread). Indeed, her mouth is beautiful. It is beautifully shaped and enticing to her man. There is some question, because of the unusual Hebrew word used here for "mouth," whether Solomon has in view physical or verbal pleasures which come from her mouth. An either/or decision is unnecessary. "Her mouth is . . . a fertile oasis with lovely words flowing out of it—not to mention possible heavy wet kissing."[4] Her lips and her words both are prizes of pleasure.

Her "brow" or temples behind the veil are compared to the halves of a pomegranate. They blushed red with desire, and the sweetness of their fruit invites Solomon to kiss them. Pomegranates were considered an aphrodisiac in the ancient world. Attractive to the eye and sweet to taste, the image appeals to the senses of both sight and taste.

Her neck was "like the tower of David constructed in layers" with the shields and weapons of Solomon's mighty men (cf. 3:7–8). She stands tall and graceful. She is neither cowed nor timid. Why should she be in the presence of a man who loves and admires her with such passion? The image "conveys a sense of unassailable strength. No man could conquer her, and her suitor is awed by the dignity she carries. Her love is a gift; it could never become plunder."[5]

Verses 5–6 draw attention to Shulammite's breasts. First, they are compared to "twins of a gazelle that feed among the lilies." They are soft and attractive, tender and delicate, making her husband want to touch and caress them gently. Second, he describes them as two mountains: one a "mountain of myrrh" and the other a "hill of frankincense." Both spices were expensive and used as perfume for the body and the marriage bed. (Prov. 7:17 informs us that the harlot perfumes her bed with myrrh, aloes, and cinnamon.) Now the senses of sight and smell are aroused. So enraptured is Solomon that he desires to make love to his wife all night long: "Before the day breaks and the shadows flee."

Time and tenderness are essential twins for a sexually and romantically attractive bedroom. Here we see that slow, romantic foreplay is underway. Solomon visually and literally, undresses his bride. He praises her specifically and in detail for everything he sees. He gives before receiving. He is as much concerned, if not more so, for her pleasure and satisfaction than he is his own. He is loving her as Christ has loved us (Eph. 5:25ff).

We really don't know what Shulammite looked like. What we do know is what she looked like to Solomon. In his eyes she was beautiful, gorgeous; no one compared to her. This bedroom is a place of satisfying attractiveness: both to Solomon and to Shulammite.

> *Come with me from Lebanon, my bride—*
>   *with me from Lebanon!*
> *Descend from the peak of Amana,*
>   *from the summit of Senir and Hermon,*
>   *from the dens of lions,*
>   *from the mountains of the leopards.*
> *You have captured my heart, my sister, my bride.*
>   *You have captured my heart with one glance of your eyes,*
>   *with one jewel of your necklace.*
> *How delightful your love is, my sister, my bride!*
> *Your love is much better than wine,*
>   *and the fragrance of your perfume than any balsam.*
> *Your lips drip sweetness like the honeycomb, my bride.*
> *Honey and milk are under your tongue.*
> *The fragrance of your garments is like the fragrance of Lebanon.*
>   *(vv. 8–11)*

LET IT BE A PLACE OF SENSUAL ANTICIPATION (vv. 8–11)

Humans are apparently the only creatures on the planet who see sex as fun. Some say possible exceptions are dolphins and pygmy chimps! Almost without exception we think about and anticipate the sexual experience. We give this area of life a lot of time and attention. Some people will order videos like Dr. Sandra Scantling's *Ordinary Couples, Extraordinary Sex,* "The sex education videos that increase sexual pleasure for both partners," advertised in major American magazines. We will attend seminars like "Getting the Love You Want," "Resexing Marriage," "Resurrecting Sex: The Passionate Marriage Approach," "Marital Sex As It Ought to Be," and "Hot Monogamy."

In the spring of 1999 many major magazines ran stories about the sensual power of chemicals called pheromones that will "boost your sex appeal and change your social and sex life forever. Science and nature's sexual secret weapon!" The high-octane potion could be ordered via a 1-888 number for $34.95 a bottle (plus $3.00 shipping and handling regardless of how many bottles you order), and with an unconditional satisfaction guarantee. "If you do not find you are meeting and dating and scoring with more people of the opposite sex after . . . 30 days, simply return the unused portion . . . for a full refund—no questions asked."

Yes, we think and talk a great deal about sex, but far too often we don't understand it, at least not as God intended. The results of going our own way have not been pretty. Perhaps God has had it right all along. When it comes to sensual anticipation, what counsel do we receive from Him?

INVITE YOUR MATE TO COME TO YOU (V. 8)

Solomon's complete attention has been on his wife. There is only one first-person reference in the first seven verses (v. 6). Biblical sex will always be focused on one's mate before it looks to one's self. Then, and only then, is it the right time to take lovemaking to the next level. Solomon has called Shulammite his "darling." Now he calls her his "bride."

He calls her to leave where she is and come to him. Lebanon was near her home. The other mountain ranges mentioned are in the general area as well. The lion's den and the mountains of the leopards perhaps represent fears Shulammite may have. He does not charge her; he calls to her. He does not demand; he invites. He invites her to leave her home and her fears behind. He will care for her. He will love her. She is his love, his darling. She is his bride, his wife. Five times in verses 8–12 Solomon refers to her as his bride. Sensual anticipation must be clothed with words of safety and security if it expects a warm reception. Solomon's invitation is beautifully delivered.

INDICATE HOW YOUR MATE CAPTIVATES YOU (VV. 9–11)

It would seem that Shulammite responded in a positive manner to Solomon's invitation. Solomon's words in verses 9–11 would seem to affirm this. He begins by saying Shulammite has "captured" or "ravished" his heart. Her love was so overpowering that he could not resist her. Her love had captured his heart, and he could not escape. Just a glance of her eye or seeing one link in her necklace sent him swooning out of control. She was enchanting, and he was powerless to resist her spell.

Solomon then says something that is very strange to our ears. He again calls Shulammite his "bride," but he also refers to her as his "sister," something he does no less than five times (cf. 4:9–10, 12; 5:1–2). Again we must understand the use of the word in its historical context. In the Ancient Near East *sister* was a term of affection and friendship. In addition to its literal meaning, it could indicate a close and intimate relationship that a husband and wife enjoyed. True lovers will also be true friends, even best friends. This is something Solomon understood well.

Repetition is often a wonderful teacher, and in verse 10 Solomon again calls Shulammite his sister, his bride. He tells her that her love is delightful and that it is "much better than wine." Wine is intoxicating and sweet, but it could not compare to this. He was drunk with love for her. Charles Spurgeon, the great British preacher of the nineteenth century, said her love was better than wine because it: (1) could be enjoyed without question, (2) would never turn sour, (3) would never produce ill effects, and (4) produced a sacred exhilaration.[6]

Her smell also got Solomon's attention. The fragrance or scent of this woman was superior to "all spices" (v. 11 NKJV). For a man, sight is closely followed by smell in the sensual realm. Shulammite knew this, and so she prepared herself in a way that would draw her man to her (not that he probably needed much encouragement).

Verse 11 moves us into even greater sensual and romantic territory. Her lips, he says, "drip sweetness like the honeycomb," and "honey and milk are under your tongue." The idea that a particular kind of kissing began in France is put to rest by this verse! Deep, wet, sweet, and passionate kissing is at least as old as this Song. Canaan was a land of milk and honey (cf. Exod. 3:8). It was a land of joy, blessing, and satisfaction that God graciously provided for the nation of Israel. It was a land of sweetness to a people who had been enslaved for more than four hundred years. Solomon found immeasurable joy in the deep, long, and intimate kisses of his bride.

Besides smelling good herself, she also applied attractive fragrances to her clothes. Lebanon flourished with cedar trees (cf. 1 Kings 5:6; Ps. 29:5; 92:12; 104:16; Isa. 2:13; 14:8; Hos. 14:5–6). The fresh aroma of those mountain cedars filled the

nostrils of Solomon as he undressed his bride and made preparation for lovemaking. Virtually all the senses—taste, touch, smell,
sight, and sound—have played a role in this sensual symphony in
this bedroom. The lovemaking which we enjoy will only be
enhanced as we follow this example.

> *My sister, my bride, is a locked garden—*
> > *a locked garden and a sealed spring.*
> *Your branches are a paradise of pomegranates*
> > *with choicest fruits,*
> > *henna with nard—*
> > *nard and saffron, calamus and cinnamon,*
> > *with all the trees of frankincense,*
> > *myrrh and aloes,*
> > *with all the best spices.*
> *You are a garden spring,*
> > *a well of flowing water*
> > *streaming from Lebanon. (vv. 12–15)*

LET IT BE A PLACE OF SPECIFIC AVAILABILITY (vv. 12–15)

One of the greatest gifts a person can give a mate in marriage
is exclusive and exciting sex. To enter marriage as a virgin is indeed
a precious treasure to bestow on a spouse. Unfortunately, it is also
a rare treasure. The Bible is crystal clear on the issue: any sex
outside of marriage is sin in the eyes of God. This includes premarital sex, extramarital sex, or unnatural sex (such as homo-
sexuality and bestiality). "Flee sexual immorality" (1 Cor. 6:18) is
God's command, and a wise person will always listen to God.

Shulammite had listened to the voice of her God concerning her sexuality. Note the beautiful imagery Solomon uses to describe his bride on their wedding night.

GOD IS PLEASED WHEN WE KEEP OURSELVES PURE (V. 12)

Shulammite is described as "a locked garden," and "a sealed spring." Each pictures her purity and virginity. She had sealed up herself for her husband. She had saved a precious treasure that belonged only to him. I have never known a woman, or a man for that matter, who ever regretted saving sex for marriage. I have, however, known many who regretted not doing so. In particular, I think of a letter written to Josh McDowell years ago that probably expresses the regrets of many scarred by the sexual revolution.

> *Dear Mr. McDowell,*
>
> *Having premarital sex was the most horrifying experience of my life. It wasn't at all the emotionally satisfying experience the world deceived me into believing. I felt as if my insides were being exposed and my heart left unattended. I know God has forgiven me of this haunting sin, but I also know I can never have my virginity back. I dread the day that I have to tell the man I truly love and wish to marry that he is not the only one—though I wish he were. I have stained my life—a stain that will never come out.*
>
> *Monica*

God is pleased, we are protected, and a mate is honored when we keep ourselves pure.

GOD IS PLEASED WHEN WE GIVE EACH OTHER PLEASURE (VV. 13–15)

Solomon extended the imagery of the garden in verses 13–14, describing his bride as an exotic array of fruits, flowers, plants, trees, and spices. She was unique and valuable, rare and desirable. She was a fantasy garden, a lover's dream. To find pomegranates, henna flowers, nard, saffron, calamus, cinnamon, frankincense, myrrh, aloes, and all the best spices in one garden was unimaginable, and yet in his bride he found them all. She would satisfy his sense of taste, sight, and smell. He could never be bored. He would enjoy the multiple pleasures discovered in this garden. Each time would be an exciting time, a new and different adventure.

Solomon now thinks of "his wife" as "a garden spring, a well of flowing water streaming from Lebanon." To other men she was locked up, enclosed, and sealed. For her husband she is wide open, accessible, and available. Indeed, her love is overflowing and streaming for him. What she once held back from others she now gives to her husband with unreserved passion and abandonment. And why? Because she had saved herself for this day and this man. She was no casualty of sexual promiscuity. She did not have the wounds of a young twenty-one year old who said with pain and sadness in her voice, "I have had 17 partners—too many, I think."[7] Purity and pleasure go hand in hand when it comes to sex. Be specific in your availability. It is worth the wait.

> *Awaken, north wind—*
> *come, south wind.*
> *Blow upon my garden,*
> *and spread the fragrance of its spices.*

Let my love come into his garden
    and eat its choicest fruits.

I have come to my garden—my sister, my bride.
I gather my myrrh with my spices.
I eat my honeycomb with my honey.
I drink my wine with my milk. (vv. 4:16–5:1a)

LET IT BE A PLACE OF SEXUAL AFFECTION (VV. 4:16–5:1A)

What do happy couples say about sex? *Reader's Digest* ran an article that answers that question with the caption, "With a dash of surprise, a pinch of romance and a word or two at the right moment, love can be kept simmering even in the longest marriage." Adapting their list slightly and adding a couple of other suggestions, I think at least twelve things can be said.

What Happy Couples Say About Sex
1. They make sex a priority; it is important to them.
2. They make time for sex.
3. They stay emotionally intimate.
4. They know how to touch and what works.
5. They keep romance alive by meeting each other's needs.
6. They keep their sexual anticipation alive.
7. They know how to play and foreplay (both in and out of bed).
8. They know how to talk to each other.
9. They remain lovers and friends.
10. They maintain a sense of humor and know how to laugh.

11. They want to please each other.

12. They cherish each other as a sacred and precious gift of God.[8]

Shulammite and Solomon certainly intended to fall in the "happy couple" category when it came to their sex lives. For the first time in our passage, Shulammite speaks, and her words would have gotten her husband's attention immediately.

ENCOURAGE YOUR MATE TO MAKE LOVE WITH YOU (V. 16)

In beautiful and enticing poetry, Shulammite invites Solomon to make love to her. She who has twice said not to awaken love until the right time (cf. 2:7; 3:5) now says, "The time is right. I am yours. Come and take me." North winds are strong and south winds more gentle. In lovemaking Shulammite wants and needs both, sometimes at the same time and sometimes at different times.

She has been listening to every word spoken by her husband, for she picks up on the imagery of the garden. She is that garden, and her love is welcome to come in and enjoy. She invites him, she guides him, she tells him what she is feeling and what she wants. Great sex is the result of good communication. All the physiological parts fit when a man and woman come together, but sex is no mere mechanical union. It is a personal and spiritual union nurtured by careful communication. We cannot be certain of all that is meant by the imagery of coming to the garden and tasting the choice fruits. It is not difficult to imagine all sorts of good stuff!

Encourage Your Mate After Love with You (v. 1)

The marriage has been consummated. The couple has made love. They were not disappointed. They had planned for it, saved themselves for it, studied up on it, and talked about it. All of their time and effort has been rewarded.

Shulammite invites Solomon to come to "his" garden in 4:16. Now in 5:1 he calls her "my" garden. In fact, nine times in this one verse he uses the word *my.* Don't miss that it is used in this manner after, not before, their lovemaking. In tender words he calls Shulammite his garden, his sister, and his bride. Coming in to her was indeed a garden delight. She smelled good, tasted good, and felt good; and he told her so. Their lovemaking had been good. It had been wonderful. She invited him to come to her and he did. He no doubt hopes for many more times together just like this, and so he romantically and tenderly expresses the pleasure she has given him.

In a study by Susan Sprecher, Ph.D., a professor of sociology at Illinois State University, sexual satisfaction was greater in relationships in which partners initiated equally or in which women sometimes initiated sex. Why then, do so many couples fall in the pattern of the man being the only one to suggest having sex? Sprecher and other sex researchers speculate that society's norms suggest that men should pursue and women should be pursued. The result may be that women tend to be less comfortable initiating sex. Or it may be that women tend to use subtle, indirect cues— which may not be consciously noticed—to initiate sexual activity, while men use more direct verbal requests and other measures. Women who initiate sex frequently are often very sexually satisfied to begin with, Sprecher believes, and this enables them to be more at ease about expressing their sexual desires. A woman who initiates sex also often stimulates her partner's sex drive and his desire for her, which helps drive this entire pattern. Several studies have found that many men like it when their female partner initiates sex. Matt Sess, 39, of New York City, says that he has always been the primary initiator in his relationship with Laura, his wife of eight years. "But when she initiates sex, it's definitely a turn-on," he says. "It doesn't happen a lot, but when it does, it's a pleasant surprise."[9]

No doubt Solomon found Shulammite to be something of a turn-on, and he let her know it—a wise man indeed.

Eat, friends!
Drink! Be intoxicated with love! (v. 1b)

LET IT BE A PLACE OF SPIRITUAL APPROVAL (V. 1B)

The last part of verse 1 has created quite a bit of interpretive discussion. Exactly who is it that encourages this man and woman in their lovemaking? Some believe it is the friends of the couple. However, the intimate knowledge of this speaker of all that has transpired in their bedroom would rule this out. Others believe it to be the voice of the wind again, personified from 4:16. Clearly, it cannot be either Solomon or Shulammite, for they are the ones being addressed.

Though His name never appears directly in the entire Song of Solomon, I believe the one who speaks here is God. He is the unseen but present guest in their bedroom. He has observed all that has happened this night, and He tells us what He thinks about it all.

SEX IN MARRIAGE ENJOYS DIVINE APPROVAL

"Eat, friends! Drink! Be intoxicated with love!" The love shared by Solomon and Shulammite, together with the gift of sex, was given to them by God.

> He lifts His voice and gives hearty approval to the entire night. He vigorously endorses and affirms the love of this couple. He takes pleasure in what has taken place. He is glad they have drunk deeply of the fountain of love. Two of His own have experienced love in all the beauty and fervor and purity that He intended for them. In fact, He urges them on to more. . . . That is his attitude toward the giving of their love to each other. And by the way, that's also His attitude toward couples today.[10]

Yes, God is there, and He is pleased with what He sees. "He sees the passion. He hears the sighs of delight. He watches the lovers as they caress each other in the most intimate places. He is witness to the fleshly, earthly sights, sounds, and smells. . . . God desires for us to rejoice in our sensuousness, to give in to it."[11]

SPOUSES ENJOY DIVINE AFFECTION

A term of tender affection flows from the mouth of God as He looks upon the couple enjoying His good gift of sex as He intended. He calls them "friends." God loves them, and He loves what He sees. How foreign this is to so many persons' thinking when they try to imagine what the Creator thinks about sex! He loves us, and He likes it when we are engaged in the passion of lovemaking within the covenant of marriage. It can be revolutionary and transforming when we accurately and correctly get the Creator's perspective. We can become like a woman named Beth who said:

> Loving my husband can become an act of worship to God. As my husband and I lie together, satiated in the afterglow of sexual ecstasy, the most natural thing in the world is for me to offer thanksgiving to my God for the beauty, the glory of our sexual joy. I don't even think about what I am doing; my heart just turns to the Lord and offers praise. Truly His gift of sex is a wondrous thing.[12]

Some men need a little assistance in preparing for romance, and so I have included an adaptation of Jody Dillow's "Lover's Quotient Test" for husbands and wives to take together. As you will see, I will advise you both not to take the results too seriously, but do take them seriously enough. The scale runs from 0 to 360. I confess that the first time I took it I made 90. (You can look up the results yourself!) Since then, I have progressed to a 170 and recently a 220. Believe me, progress has been made in more than one area! I was motivated to get to work after giving this silly test one time at a marriage conference in Lawton, Oklahoma. The next night a beautiful and elegant lady in her late forties or early fifties came up to me to tell me the score her husband had achieved on the test. Her pastor later told me this was perhaps the finest and godliest woman he had ever known. Well, her husband scored a 270! To this date that is still the highest first-time score I've seen recorded. As you might suspect by now, I am a rather playful person, and so I said, "I have only one thing more to ask. Is he really that good?" I will never forget her response. She said, "Yes, he is. I am certain that I am married to the most wonderful man in all the world." And with those words she kindly and graciously walked away.

God spoke to my heart that night through that precious lady. I began to think, *Wouldn't it be wonderful, if someone were to ask my wife, Charlotte, "Is Danny that good?" and with honesty and integrity she could say, "Yes, he is. I'm certain I am married to the most wonderful man in all the world."* Few things could be said about a man, a husband, by his wife, that would be a greater honor than that. So guys, don't take the test too seriously, but do take it seriously enough. If you will, you will find that the beauty and the blessings of the Christian bedroom will be so much more than you would have ever imagined.

Lover's Quotient Test

We need to find out just how creative you are as a husband! Let's take the following Lover's Quotient Test. Give yourself ten points for each item on the following list if you have done it once in the past six months. If you have done any item on the list two or more times, you get twenty points. Once again: don't take the results too seriously, but do take them seriously enough!

_____ Have you phoned her during the week and asked her out for one evening that weekend without telling her where you are taking her? A mystery date is what we have in mind!

_____ Have you given her an evening completely off? You clean up the kitchen; you take care of the kids; you get things settled for the night.

_____ Have you gone parking with her at some safe and secluded spot and kissed and talked for an evening?

_____ Have you drawn a bath for her after dinner? Put a scented candle in the bathroom; added bath oil to the bath; sent her there right after dinner, and then you cleaned up and put the kids to bed while she relaxed? (In order to get any points for this you must also clean up the tub!)

_____ Have you phoned her from work to tell her you were thinking nice thoughts about her? (You get no points for this one if you asked her what was in the mail or what is for dinner!)

_____ Have you written her a love letter and sent it special delivery? (First class mail will do.)

_____ Have you made a tape recording of all the reasons you have for loving her? Given it to her wrapped in a sheer negligee?

____ Have you given her a day off? Sent her out to
do what she wants? You clean the house, fix the
meals, and take care of the kids. (My wife says
you ought to get thirty points for this one!)

____ Have you put a special-effects recording of
ocean waves on tape and played it while
you had a luau on the living room floor?
Other creative evening adventures may be
substituted!

____ Have you spent a whole evening (more than
two hours) sharing mutual goals and planning
family objectives with her and the children?

____ Have you ever planned a surprise weekend?
You make the reservations and arrange for
someone to keep the children for two days. Tell
her to pack her suitcase, but don't tell her
where you are going (just be sure it's not the
Super Bowl). Make it someplace romantic.

____ Have you picked up your clothes just one time
in the past six months and put them on hangers?

____ Have you given her an all-over body massage
with scented lotion? (If not, why not?)

____ Have you spent a session of making love to her
that included at least two hours of romantic
conversation, shared dreams, and much variety
of approach and caresses?

____ Have you repaired something around the house that she has not requested?

____ Have you kissed her passionately for at least thirty seconds one morning just before you left for work or one evening when you walked in the door?

____ Have you brought her an unexpected little gift like perfume, a ring, or an item of clothing?

____ Have you replaced her old negligee?

This ridiculous test has been given to men all over the country. Let's see how your scores compare with theirs:

200–360	Lover	Awesome! You are the man! You undoubtedly have one of the most satisfied wives in the country. You are in the top one percent!
150–200	Good	Way to go! Very few make this category. You are a top-ten candidate! Your wife probably smiles a lot!
100–150	Average	This husband is the norm and usually not very exciting as a lover. You are steady, but there are not many fireworks in the area of romance from your wife's perspective.

50–100	Klutz	Boring! You can do better than this! Too many score in this category. I hope you will begin to work to move up soon.
0–50	Typical Husband	Ouch! Sad! Sad! Sad! There is a huge difference between a *typical* husband and a *lover*. The only reason your wife is still married to you is that she's a Christian. She has unusual capacity for unconditional acceptance (of you!), and some verses in the Bible sustain her.

Adapted from Jody Dillow's "Lover's Quotient Test."

Chapter 9

How to Avoid a Bad Night in the Bedroom

THE SONG OF SONGS 5:2–8

"Lawyers can't cope as divorce epidemic sweeps the United Kingdom," reported the *London Observer*, January 9, 2000. An outbreak of "matrimonial millennial madness" led one of Britain's leading divorce law firms, Lloyd Platts & Co., to refuse to take on any new clients. Said Vanessa Lloyd Platts, "If couples continue to separate at the current rate, there won't be anybody left to divorce in 10 years." Feminist writer Natasha Walter argued, "This means people don't want to put up with second best anymore! Marriage isn't keeping up with the way we conduct our relationships and what I see much more of is that a lot of men and women are looking for love but not necessarily within the framework of one partner for life." Julia Cole, a spokesperson for the counseling organization Relate, said that the beginning of a new century had prompted a new scrutiny of relationships. Sexual problems, always uppermost in people's minds, seem especially widespread. "There is an expectation that along with the perfect lunch, the perfect presents, the perfect New Year's Eve, there will be lovely, perfect sex. The contrast between expectations and reality is often enormous."[1]

Obviously, far too many people are experiencing significant disappointment with their marriage, and problems often find their way into the bedroom. Most problems in a marriage do not *begin* in the bedroom, but many problems in a marriage do *end up* in the bedroom. And no marriage will be all that God intended if the intimate life is not meaningful, satisfying, and enjoyable.

Proverbs 5:18 says, "Let your fountain be blessed, and take pleasure in the wife of your youth." Notice it did not say *"only in your youth"!* In February 1999, the *National Health and Social Life Survey* completed what was identified as the most comprehensive study of American sex lives ever. The results were published in *JAMA* with some interesting findings.[2]

1. Sexually active singles have the most sexual problems and get the least pleasure out of sex.
2. Men with the most "liberal attitudes about sex" are seventy-five percent more likely to fail to satisfy their partners.
3. Married couples by far reported the happiest satisfaction with their sex lives.
4. The most sexually satisfied demographic group of them is that of married couples between fifty and fifty-nine!

Oh, but the news gets even better. A November 29, 1999 news release noted:

When University of Chicago researchers set out to discover which religious denominations have the best sex they learned that the faithful don't do all their shouting in church. Conservative Protestant women,

their 1994 survey found, report by far the most
orgasms: 32% say they achieve orgasm every time they
make love. Mainline protestants and Catholics lagged
five points behind. Those with no religious affiliation
were at 22%. (Unitarians may not wish to read any
further.)

Newsweek may run a story that asks: "Was it virtually good
for you? Sex: the best lovemaking of your life is now just a few
nanobots and a body suit away," touting the virtues of techno,
virtual-reality sex![3] And *Cosmopolitan* may challenge us with
"Cosmo's 20 Favorite Sex Tips Ever," which claims, "We have the
wall-shaking, earth-quaking moves that'll make your bed end up
across the room."[4] However, if you really are interested in the
best sex possible, based on the data, find you a born-again babe
and keep her around because in your fifties the best is yet to
come!

However, it is still the case that too many couples are suffering
the hurt and disappointment of too many bad nights in the bedroom. When those bad nights come, what do we do? How should
we respond? Might I offer a suggestion: let's follow the Bible,
God's Word. Let's allow God to provide guidance on how we can
avoid bad nights in the bedroom.

> *I sleep, but my heart is awake.*
> *A sound! My love is knocking!*
> *Open to me, my sister, my darling,*
> *my dove, my perfect one.*
> *For my head is drenched with dew,*
> *my hair with droplets of the night. (v. 2)*

THE DESIRE FOR LOVE MAY FAIL BECAUSE
OF BAD TIMING (V. 2)

Shulammite, Solomon's wife, is in bed. Perhaps she is dreaming or half awake, tossing and turning out of anxiety and disappointment. The issue is simple: he is late again. The flow of the text hints that she may have been hoping for, or expecting, a night of romantic intimacy with her love, her husband. However, he was out again, and he was late. Her desires had been dashed. Why did this happen? What can be the cause of a bad night in the bedroom?

WORK MAY CAUSE THE PROBLEM

The Bible says, "His head is drenched with dew," and his "hair with droplets of the night." This is an example of Hebrew parallelism. The point is clear. It was late, near or after midnight. Like many men he probably had to work late. Struggling to make things come together in the tough, cruel world of a king required long hard days. Sometimes those days turned into nights. Time is, and has always been, our most precious commodity. You can only spend it *one time* and at *one place.* On this particular evening *work* won out over the *wife,* and the stage is set for a confrontation, a showdown in the bedroom.

WORDS MAY NOT CURE THE PROBLEM

In the Ancient Near East, it was the custom for a husband and wife to occupy separate bedrooms. What a terrible idea! Solomon has come home and is tired, but he is not too tired. He was, after all, a man! The fact is he was probably in need of both emotional and physical support and intimacy with his wife after a long, hard day. This is how God has wired a man. A study notes that

> for men the secret of a happy marriage is emotional
> support and an active sex life. While women would
> just like their husbands to take more interest in them.
> . . . Women said, they just wanted husbands to take a
> greater interest in their opinions and a more active
> role in their social lives. Marriage counselor Sheron Li
> Yuet-Yi said, "sex plays an essential role in building up
> a successful marriage. We have seen newlyweds who
> do not have any idea how to do it and we have some
> middle-aged couples who are either too lazy or too
> tired."[5]

Sometimes things just don't come together as we had hoped in the bedroom.

Solomon's approach with his wife is gentle and sensitive. Perhaps he sensed some tension. A locked door to the bedroom might tip a guy off! Note his four names of affection and the four uses of the possessive pronoun *my*:

My sister (cf. 4:9) emphasizes their friendship and the permanency of their relationship.

My darling (cf. 1:9; used nine times and always by Solomon) speaks of the one in whom I delight and take pleasure. It is often used in the context of acknowledging her beauty.

My dove (cf. 2:14) was perhaps a pet name. It describes her gentleness.

My perfect one means "my flawless or blameless one,"
the one whom I know is wholly mine and no other's.

I am convinced that Solomon is sincere in his compliments
and words of praise. Of course this is not always the case with husbands, and our wives can become experts in deciphering some of
our code phrases. A radio station in Louisville had some fun at
males' expense when they talked about "what men really mean
when they say . . ."

> "It's a guy thing," really means, "There is no rational
> thought pattern connected with it, and you have no
> chance at all of making it logical."

> "Can I help with dinner?" really means, "Why isn't it
> already on the table?"

> "Uh-huh," "sure, honey," or "yes, dear," really means
> absolutely nothing; it's a conditioned male response.

> "It would take too long to explain," really means,
> "I have no idea how it works."

> "We're going to be late," really means, "Now I have a
> legitimate excuse to drive like a maniac."

> "Take a break, honey, you're working too hard," really
> means, "I can't hear the game over the vacuum cleaner."

> "That's interesting, dear," really means, "Are you still
> talking?"

"That's women's work," really means, "It's difficult,
dirty, and thankless."

"We share the housework," really means, "I make the
messes; she cleans them up."

"You know how bad my memory is," really means,
"I remember the theme song to *F Troop,* the address of
the first girl I ever kissed, and the vehicle identification
number of every car I've ever owned, but I forgot your
birthday."

"Oh, don't fuss. I just cut myself. It's no big deal," really
means, "I have severed a limb but will bleed to death
before I admit that I am hurt."

"Hey, I've got my reasons for what I am doing," really
means, "And I sure hope I think of some pretty soon."

"I can't find it," really means, "When I look in the
refrigerator, I can't move the milk jug because if the
ketchup is not behind it then the milk jug won!"

"What did I do this time?" really means, "What did you
catch me doing?"

"I heard you," really means, "I haven't the foggiest clue
what you just said, and I am desperately hoping that
I can fake it well enough so that you don't spend the
next three days yelling at me."

No, sometimes words, even our best ones, cannot overcome bad timing and prevent a bad night in the bedroom.

> *I have taken off my clothing.*
> > *How can I put it back on?*
> *I have washed my feet.*
> > *How can I get them dirty? (v. 3)*

THE DETAILS FOR LOVE MAY FEEL LIKE TOO MUCH TROUBLE (V. 3)

Shulammite was perhaps mad, certainly hurt. The most basic needs of her heart had not been met. Bob Turnbull, in "What Your Wife Really Needs," reminds us guys that our wives will dry up and wither on the inside without four things:

Time—the currency of a relationship; clearing space in your calendar for her says you are valuable to me.

Talk—this is how she connects with you. It is also one way in which she handles stress (men on the other hand, walk or take flight).

Tenderness—it feeds her soul when she is nourished and knows she is cherished.

Touch—non-sexual, affectionate touch is crucial to a wife, and if she only receives it as the pre-game to sex, she will begin to feel used, like a marital prostitute.[6]

Whether he meant to or not, and he probably didn't, Solomon failed this *four-T* test, at least in the eyes of his wife.

This, however, does not justify how Shulammite responds, and her response is selfish and especially insensitive to the fragility of the male ego. An evening that once held promise for both the husband and the wife is about to go down the drain. What can we do to avoid this?

GUARD AGAINST SILLY PRIORITIES

Her response in twenty-first-century America would translate, "Not tonight; I have a headache." "Not tonight; I'm too tired." Several Bible teachers note that "I have taken off my clothing" suggests she now lay naked, unclothed beneath the sheets. Is there perhaps a little dig hinting at "what you will miss because you stayed out too late"? I like, as a better response, what one man shared: "My wife decided to put a spark back into our marriage. Knowing how tired she gets at the end of the day, she prearranged a solution to a potential problem. When I came to bed, I found this note on my pillow: 'I'm feeling romantic. If I'm asleep, wake me up and remind me.'" In essence Shulammite says: "My comfort is more important than your needs or desires. I waited; it's late. So sad. Too bad. If you can't get home at a decent hour, don't expect any special attention from me."

GUARD AGAINST BEING A SELFISH PERSON

Washing the feet was an oriental custom before eating a meal or retiring for bed. Shulammite was washed up and ready for bed. To have to get up, put on her clothes, and get her feet dirty was too much trouble. Self-centeredness is a deadly sin. It can and will destroy anything that gets in its path. It is also foolish because it never has a truly accurate picture of reality.

In this context let me address one new and specific danger to our marriages that has recently come onto the scene. Computers are one of the marvelous inventions of the twentieth century. They have produced much good in many areas of life. Marriages, however, have suffered far too often from pornography, cybersex, and illusionary and unreal on-line romancing. In "Letters of the Century: America 1900–1999," 412 letters were compiled to show us something about our personal perspectives during the twentieth century. The last letter selected came from the Shirley Glass AOL Electra Column. It was picked because it captured best the last decade and illustrated how the complexities of the computer age have changed us. It reads as follows:

> Dear Dr. Glass,
> I met a very interesting man online a couple of weeks
> ago and have talked to him on the phone several times
> as well. He is enchanting, charming, and everything
> I could possibly want. The trouble is that I'm already
> married and all the way across the country from
> Mr. Wonderful. I really think I love this man, but what
> can I do?
> Sincerely,
>
> Confused and Charmed.

Listen also to Shirley's wise and direct counsel.

> Dear Confused and Charmed,
> Your "Mr. Wonderful" may be somebody else's phi-
> landering husband. Internet relationships create a

romantic mystique because you can create exciting
fantasies about the other person. Add a little dose of
secrecy, emotional intimacy, and sexual innuendoes,
and you've got a full-blown emotional affair. It is easy
to be charming when you are not dealing with the
everyday irritations of leaking roofs and noisy kids.
The love that you feel for this man is based on
romantic idealization, whereas your marriage is based
on reality. Furthermore, stable long-term relationships are seldom as exciting as stage 1 (the honey-
moon) relationships. What does your online search
for companionship and romance indicate about your
marriage? Talk to your husband about your wants and
needs and try to put some energy back into your
marriage.

Selfishness and self-centeredness are death to a relationship.
They will never build up but only tear down. Selfishness is unre-
alistic. It is harmful. It is sin. And it is almost always filled with
regret. Self-centeredness is certain to produce a bad night in the
bedroom and potentially many lonely ones as well.

My love thrust his hand through the opening,
and my feelings were stirred for him.
I rose to open for my love.
My hands dripped with myrrh,
my fingers with flowing myrrh
on the handles of the bolt.
I opened to my love,
but my love had turned and gone away.

I was crushed that he had left.
I sought him, but did not find him.
I called him, but he did not answer.
The guards who go about the city found me.
They beat and wounded me;
   they took my cloak from me—
   the guardians of the walls. (vv. 4–7)

THE DENIAL OF LOVE MAY FLOWER ONLY TEMPORARILY (VV. 4–7)

Six times in verses 2–8 Shulammite calls Solomon "my love." She does so four more times in verses 9–10. She has been angry with him, but she does love him. His tender words have worked their way into her heart. Now Solomon, being the typical male, follows up with one last advance. He gently places his hand on the latch (the opening of the door). Because of the poetic, symbolic, and erotic nature of this book, numerous scholars have noted the male hand is sometimes used euphemistically for the sexual parts of a man (cf. Isa. 57:8, 10; Jer. 5:31; 50:15). If this is so, the latch or opening corresponds most certainly to the female counterpart. What is the response to this kind, sensitive, and sensual overture?

YOU MAY RECONSIDER SAYING NO (VV. 4–5)

Her "feelings were stirred" for her husband. She is touched by his kindness. With the words, "I rose," she moves into action. The "I" is emphatic. She now wants to make things right. "The myrrh" is perhaps left by Solomon as a sign of his love and regret that things had gone sour or perhaps on the hand of Shulammite who quickly prepared herself for the now desired sexual rendezvous. She wanted her man as much as he wanted her.

It is tragic that in many marriages the bedroom becomes a war zone and a battlefield because wives are convinced their husbands always want sex and husbands are convinced their wives like to say no as often as possible. A friend of mine who does marriage counseling told me about a woman who came to him because she was having marriage problems. The issue was sex. It seemed to her that sex was all her husband was interested in, 24–7, and he was constantly putting enormous pressure on her for activity in that department. She was just about at the end of her rope, and so she came looking for help.

My friend is an insightful and wise person, and he gave the lady an interesting assignment. He asked her to go back home and for the next week to become a "huntress" in her relationship with her husband. He told her to track him down again and again, several times a day if she could, and engage in sexual relations. He asked her to call him at the end of the week and tell him what the results were of this plan.

Well, my friend did not get a call at the end of the week. He received a phone call just two days later. The woman said, "I think your plan worked. My husband is lying over in the corner of our bedroom waving a white handkerchief! In fact, this whole day, when I come into a room where he is, he tries to get out as fast as he can!"

She went on to tell him that they both felt very foolish. They had, after more than fifteen years of marriage, come to realize that their sexual appetites, though not identical, were similar and definitely compatible. He was always pressuring her because he thought she always wanted to say no. If he didn't turn up the heat, they would never have sex, he thought. She, on the other hand, was in the resistance mode because she thought having sex is all he ever wants to do, and if she didn't say no at least some of the time they would be having sex all of the time. Better communication could have saved this couple years of stress and hurt. Better communication can save us from these things as well.

You May Reap Saying No (v. 6)

Studies now offer preliminary evidence that actual physical changes occur during marital conflict. For example, marital conflict affects the heart rate. These studies also show that marital fights can weaken the immune system (especially in women), raise blood pressure, and speed up the heart rate. For women, simply discussing angry feelings can lead to these stressed-out body reactions. For men the stress seems to be accompanied by the act of talking louder and faster. The greatest benefits regarding health and long life come to those who are happily married. Those who are happily married seem healthier overall than any other group.

Marital conflict has the potential for suffering and sorrow in many areas. Our text addresses two.

He may walk. It has been well said, "More belongs to marriage than four bare legs in a bed." Though men like that idea, their needs run much deeper. Yvonne Turnbull, in "What Your Husband Really Wants" notes four things a husband longs to receive from his wife:

Being his cheerleader—A man thrives on his wife's approval and praise.

Being his champion—A wife's respect and encouragement lifts a man's spirit and his sense of self-worth.

Being his companion—A man wants his wife to be his
best friend.

Being his complement—A woman is necessary to complete a man.[7]

A single friend of mine says, "Being single makes for lonely
nights but peaceful days." A married man longs for both *peaceful
days* and *intimate nights*. If he does not receive them, he may walk
away (withdraw) or even out of the relationship. Such was
Solomon's response on this occasion.

He may not talk. "Wounded males almost always go into a
shell." Most husbands will not fight their wives physically or ver
bally. They walk and they won't talk. Marriage counselor Howard
Markman has said, "Men don't want to spend their lives fighting,
so they start withdrawing. That's a typical pattern of development
of marital distress."

YOU MAY REGRET SAYING NO (V. 7)

This verse should be taken symbolically of Shulammite's own
disappointment in herself. It is the pain she feels not from her
mate, but from *herself* and, I believe, from *God's Spirit*. If our
spouse hurts us, wrongs us, we should give God some time to
work in his or her heart. He will always do a much better job.

You may be alone. John Gottman, a nationally respected marriage counselor and professor of psychology at the University of
Washington, says men and women kill their love with *criticism*,

contempt, defensiveness, stonewalling, and the failure to repair the hurt caused by these harsh styles. When these unhelpful strategies for dealing with disappointment are not corrected, people commonly end up alone.

You may be ashamed. Her cloak (or veil) is taken away. She feels as if everything valuable and important to her is gone. Why? Because God has worked in her heart. Distance has made the heart grow fonder. Without the interference of a griping, whining, and nagging mate, the Lord had done what only He can do. The stage is now set for reconciliation and reunion.

> *Young women of Jerusalem, I charge you:*
>   *if you find my love,*
>   *tell him that I am lovesick. (v. 8)*

THE DRIVE OF LOVE MAY FLAME WITH TESTIMONY (V. 8)

"The young women of Jerusalem" comprise the chorus group that appears throughout the book at strategic times. They are called by Shulammite and charged as solemn witnesses to what she is about to say. These will be important words, words from the heart and words she hopes will be trumpeted throughout the land.

TELL OTHERS OF YOUR LOVE

Here are the right *words* from the right *heart* at the right *time* and, yes, to the right *persons.* She is his *cheerleader,* and he is her *champion.* This speaks loudly to his male ego, to who and what he is as a man on the inside. Herbert Stein raises the issue, "why a man needs a woman" and writes: (1) She is a warm body in bed to cuddle and comfort. (2) She provides intimate conversation (interest, understanding and trust). (3) She serves his need to be needed. "To this woman you are irreplaceable at any price."[8]

In the context of sex, Douglas Wilson, in *Reforming Marriage*, says, "There is a sexual relationship at the center of the home which should be obvious to all who live there—hugs, kisses, and romantic attention. . . . There is nothing wrong with children knowing that their father is male and their mother is female and that they have a sexual relationship. There is something wrong with them not knowing."[9]

TELL YOUR MATE OF YOUR LOVE

It has been said, "The opposite of love is indifference." Alphonse Kerr says, "Love is the most terrible, and also the most generous, of the passions; it is the only one which includes in its dreams the happiness of someone else." Shulammite is saying in verse 8: "I can't last another day without you. Am I too weak or disinterested to make love to him? Don't be foolish. How could I not want more? I have lovesickness. The only remedy is him!"

"In marriage, the eye finds, the heart chooses, the hand binds and only death should loose." Psychologist Howard Markman, speaking at Duquesne University in October 1999 said, "It's not how much you love each other, but when conflicts arise, [it's] how you handle them that determines the success of your marriage or relationship." George Worgul, associate director of Duquesne's Family Institute and a theology professor, added, "Many people want to have good relationships and enjoy a happy marriage. Love, however, is hard work."

They're right. Love is hard work, but it is worthwhile work. And when the work is pursued following God's guidelines and for His glory, you'll enjoy a Christian marriage and discover a Christian bedroom—one that is satisfying, liberated, sensual, erotic, intimate, and pleasing both to God and each other. With a commitment to Jesus and each other, and the courage to stay with it no matter what, we can find the joy God planned.

Chapter 10

Put Your Husband Where Your Heart Is and When a Man Loves a Woman

THE SONG OF SONGS 5:9–6:13

Marriage is scary business to many people today. With so many unhappy couples sharing horror stories, some persons will do almost anything to increase their odds for success. In New York some women are enrolling in a class called "Marriage Works," a six-month, 276-hour course to help them land the right mate. The cost is a cool $9,600.[1] To this class you can add the Divorce Busting Center's Keeping Love Alive workshop; the Hot Monogamy workshop (four days, $1,800 per couple/$1,000 per person); Twogether, Inc.'s Pairs Passage to Intimacy (two days, $499 per couple/$250 per person); Getting the Love You Want: Workshop for Couples (two days, $575 per couple); and Pairs for Love's Language of Love (one day, $25); If You Really Loved Me (one day, $225 per couple/$125 per person); and Passage to Intimacy Weekend (two days, $450 per couple/$250 per person). I guess desperate times call for desperate measures.

God did not intend for marriage to end quickly. He did not intend for it to be painfully endured. He intended it to be wonderfully enjoyed. It was not His plan that it would be a burden. He wants it to be a blessing. In order for us to experience maximum marriage satisfaction, it is essential that we grow to know each other. A woman must come to understand the unique needs her husband has as a man. A man must discover the unique needs his wife has as a woman. All of this is hard work, lifelong work, but work that pays unbelievably rich dividends.

In marriage, a wife needs to put her husband where her heart is. A man, on the other hand, needs to love his wife, love his woman. We do this by learning to meet some basic needs that are the essence of who our mate is. For a man there are at least five. For a woman there are at least seven.[2] Let's begin looking at these and see what we might learn.

> *My love is fit and strong,*
> > *notable among ten thousand.*
> *His head is purest gold,*
> > *his hair is wavy*
> > *and black as a raven.*
> *His eyes are like doves*
> > *beside streams of water,*
> > *washed in milk*
> > *and set like jewels.*
> *His cheeks are like beds of spice,*
> > *towers of perfume.*
> *His lips are lilies,*
> > *dripping with flowing myrrh.*
> *His arms are rods of gold*
> > *set with topaz.*

His body is an ivory panel
   covered with sapphires.
His legs are alabaster pillars
   set on pedestals of pure gold.
His presence is like Lebanon,
   As majestic as the cedars. (5:10–15)

A WOMAN MUST PUT HER HUSBAND WHERE HER HEART IS (VV. 10–15)

Shulammite is growing in her knowledge of Solomon. Their relationship is maturing. They hit a bump in the road in 5:2–8, but they refused to let that sidetrack them. Out of that conflict they discover a better understanding of each other and a greater commitment to move ahead. What did Shulammite discover about Solomon concerning his basic needs?

HE NEEDS ADMIRATION AND RESPECT (VV. 10–15)

God has wired a man in such a way that he longs for and needs his wife's admiration and respect more than anything else (cf. Eph. 5:33b). She understands and appreciates both his value and achievements more than anyone else. She reminds him of his gifts and abilities and helps him in the area of self-confidence. She is his biggest fan, and he is her hero. She is proud of her husband not out of duty but as an expression of genuine and sincere admiration for the man she loves and with whom she has chosen to share her life. She sees her husband as a gift from God.

In his February 1995 newsletter, James Dobson provided some insightful marital counsel. In the process of challenging

both husbands and wives, he nailed this issue concerning a man's
need for admiration and respect.

> It is never too late to put a little excitement in your
> relationship. Romantic love is the fuel that powers the
> female engine. Unfortunately, most of us get so busy
> earning a living that we often drift away from the
> things that drew us together in the first place . . .
> [therefore] a gentle reminder to men: marriages must
> be nurtured or they wither like a plant without water.
> There is more than one perspective on every substan-
> tive issue, however, and we need to look at the other
> side of this one. The task of maintaining a marriage is
> not exclusively a masculine responsibility. It should be
> shared equally by men and women. Wives must under-
> stand and meet the needs of their husbands, too. That
> is an idea you may not have heard in a while. Let me be
> more specific. It is my conviction that Christian writ-
> ers, myself included, have tended to overstate the mas-
> culine responsibilities in marriage and to understate
> the feminine. Men have been criticized for their fail-
> ures at home, and yes, many of us deserve those criti-
> cisms. But women are imperfect people too and their
> shortcomings must also be addressed. One of them is
> the failure of some wives to show respect and admira-
> tion for their husbands. George Gilder, author of *Men
> and Marriage,* believes women are actually more
> important to the stability and productivity of men
> than men are to the well-being of women. I am
> inclined to agree. When a wife believes in her husband

and deeply respects him, he gains the confidence necessary to compete successfully and live responsibly. She
gives him a reason to harness his masculine energy—to
build a home, obtain and keep a job, remain sober, live
within the law, spend money wisely, etc. Without positive feminine influence, he may redirect the power of
testosterone in a way that is destructive to himself and
to society at large. . . . What should a woman do for a
man that will relate directly to his masculine nature? In
a word, she can build his confidence.[3]

My wife's approval means the world to me. Knowing that she is in
my corner, that she loves and admires me, serves both to motivate
and inspire me.

Shulammite met Solomon's need for admiration and respect
with a catalogue of praise in 5:10–15. Here she lauds both his
appearance and his character. She says, "My love is fit and strong,"
which may mean "dazzlingly ruddy."[4] "His hair is wavy and black
as a raven." He is good looking to her—tall, dark, and handsome.
"His head is purest gold" is a statement of its great wealth and
value. This is what he is to her. Her description of his eyes reflects
peace and gentleness, calmness and tranquility, brightness and
alertness. They too are attractive, "washed in milk and set like
jewels." His cheeks are sweet scented, possessing a pleasant and
desirable smell from his cologne. His lips possess sweet, wet kisses
that she longs to embrace. They are "lilies, dripping with flowing
myrrh." Her husband arouses her senses of smell and taste, and
she tells him so.

Physically he has prepared himself for her. His arms are
strong and valuable like "rods of gold." His body is handsome,

carved, and cut like ivory, "covered with sapphires." His attractiveness and worth is much to be admired, she says. His legs are strong and sturdy like "pillars set on pedestals of pure gold." His appearance is breathtaking and unimaginable, likened unto the beauty and grandeur of the tall and imposing cedar trees of Lebanon. His is a rugged attractiveness, a masculine attractiveness. Shulammite tells him he is handsome and valuable inwardly and outwardly, in appearance and character. He is the man with whom she has chosen to share and spend her life, and she has no regrets.

A woman is crucial to the success and well-being of a man. It is indeed the case that a great woman can take a mediocre man and raise him to the level of good. But a not so great woman can take a great man and pull him down to the level of mediocrity. A woman's admiration and respect for her man often provide the key and make the difference. Sandra Aldrich says women who want to be treated like queens need to treat their husbands like kings.[5]

> *His mouth is sweetness.*
> *He is absolutely desirable.*
> *This is my love, and this is my friend,*
>   *young women of Jerusalem . . . .*
>
> *My love has gone down to his garden,*
>   *to beds of spice,*
> *to feed in the gardens*
>   *and gather lilies.*
> *I am my love's and my love is mine;*
>   *he feeds among the lilies. (5:16; 6:2–3)*

HE NEEDS SEXUAL FULFILLMENT (5:16; 6:2–3)

It is no surprise to discover in survey after survey that men say sexual fulfillment is their number-one need. Now to be sure it is high on the list of a male, but I am convinced it is not number one, but number two. I am also convinced that a man's need for admiration and respect, and his need for sexual fulfillment, are intimately connected. If a woman fails to meet his need for sexual fulfillment, she will also fail to meet his need for admiration and respect. Why? Because a man finds it impossible to believe that his wife admires and respects him if she does not desire him sexually. In other words his ability to attract her and satisfy her sexually is essential to his sense of self-worth and his need for admiration and respect.

Shulammite knew this, and so she worked at becoming an expert sexual partner for Solomon. She studied her own desires and responses to recognize what brought out the best in her. She also communicated this information to her husband to ensure that their sex life would be satisfying and enjoyable. In an article entitled "Communicating About Sex Keeps Couples Loving," Dr. Maj-Britt Rosenbaum of Long Island Jewish Medical Center points out that

> opposite sexes sometimes have opposite views about sex, which can spell trouble for a relationship if it is not worked out. Experts agree it is common for people to have different sexual styles. But couples who communicate about their differences can often resolve them, while those who view opposing styles as rejection or as a lack of love are on a collision course with disaster. . . . There is no substitute for talking things out so the other person understands your feelings.

The article goes on to address areas of potential conflict such as Mr. All the Time versus Mrs. Occasionally, Planned Patti versus Spontaneous Sam, Daytime David versus Nightime Natalie, Hurry Up Harry versus Slow Down Denise, I Like the Darkness Diane versus I Love the Light Larry, and One Track Mind Michael versus Instant Distraction Donna.[6]

In the Song of Songs 5:16, Shulammite again speaks of the beauty of his mouth and the fact that he is altogether attractive. She desires him. She wants him, and again she tells him so. In her mind, who wouldn't want such a man? In 6:2–3 she says he has gone to his garden for a time of enjoyment. This is a reference to Shulammite herself (cf. 4:16), and in particular to giving herself in lovemaking. She provides for him "beds of spice," a place of pleasure. There he feeds and gathers that which satisfies and pleases him. She is available to him. She is there for his enjoyment. She desires him. The bedroom of this couple will never become a place of boredom.

Men and women do not approach sex in the same way and with the same perspective. When it comes to sex, men are like *microwave ovens* and women are like *Crock Pots*. What does this mean? Simply put, men are creatures of sight and are moved by what they see. If a man sees what he likes, like a microwave oven, he can heat up in a hurry. On the other hand, a woman must simmer a while before she will be ready! Willard Harley has said that in marriage we must create an atmosphere of affection in which sex will be enjoyed more often and with greater pleasure. Phil McGraw, author of *Relationship Rescue: A 7 Step Strategy for Reconnecting with Your Partner* says, "If you have a good sexual relationship, it's about 10% of the value of the relationship overall. If you don't have a good sexual relationship, it's about 90%."[7]

"For many people, sex has become a labor rather than an adventure."[8] However, no marriage will ever be everything God wants it to be without the beautiful gift of sex being active and satisfying for both. It requires communication and understanding. But if we will make it a priority and give it the attention it requires, we can find the full joy and satisfaction that the Song of Songs promises.

> *I am my love's and my love is mine;*
> *he feeds among the lilies. (6:3)*

HE NEEDS HOME SUPPORT (V. 3)

Shulammite expresses great confidence in the relationship she enjoys with Solomon in this verse (6:3). She says, "I am my love's and my love is mine." She also notes that he is comfortable in her presence and in their home. "He feeds among the lilies." Not only does he find her *physically* satisfying, he also finds her and their home *emotionally* satisfying. She has created a home that offers him an atmosphere of peace and quiet and refuge. She manages the home, and it is a place of rest and rejuvenation. Shulammite understood what all women need to understand: that the wife/mother is the emotional hub of the family.

A colloquial saying is well-known by almost all married persons. It goes something like this, "In the home, if Mama ain't happy, then ain't nobody happy!" This may not be fair, but it is true. It is the way that things are. I am fond of saying that a woman is the thermostat of the home. If her thermostat goes up to 90 or 95 degrees, it is not just hot for her; it is hot for everybody. On the other hand, if her thermostat goes down to 70 or 65 degrees, it is not just cool for her; it is cool for everyone.

One thing a man detests is a nagging, griping, whiny woman. God knows this and addresses it several times in the Book of Proverbs. Note the following verses:

"The woman Folly is rowdy; she is gullible and knows nothing" *(9:13).*
"A wife's nagging is an endless dripping" *(19:13).*
"Better to live on the corner of a roof, than to share a house with a nagging wife" *(21:9).*
"Better to live in a wilderness than with a nagging and hot-tempered wife" *(22:9).*

A man will not hang around a woman that is continually badgering him and beating him up verbally. Basically he will take one of two actions. Either he will fight or take flight. Most men won't fight their wives. They will not fight them physically because it is wrong, it strips away their masculinity, and they will also go to jail (and rightly so). Most men will not fight their wives verbally, either. There is a simple reason for this. They almost always lose verbal battles. Women are verbal animals. It is said that the average male speaks somewhere between ten thousand and twelve thousand words per day. On the other hand the average female speaks somewhere between twenty thousand and twenty-five thousand words per day with gusts of up to fifty thousand words! (I'm joking about the gusts!) In other words, women are well equipped for verbal battles and men are not. As a result most men will not fight their wives physically or verbally; they choose instead to take flight. They become known as workaholics or persons engaged in 1,001 extracurricular activities. The reason for all of this is simple: it is quieter alone at the office or out on a softball field. A woman must understand how crucial she is to providing a home that is a place of support for her husband. Michele Weiner-Davis, author of *Divorce Busting* and *Getting Through to the Man You Love* says, "The key to dealing with men is to stop talking and start acting. . . . Women need to learn male friendly methods of persuasion and stop doing what doesn't work." Her suggestions included:

- Stop pressing your point when it's obvious he's heard you, even if he doesn't acknowledge it.
- Make your goals clear and action-oriented.
- Pay attention to how your conflict ends.
- Ignore [some] undesirable behavior.
- Take a time-out.
- Emphasize the positive.

"It's far more efficient to praise than scold, to reward than punish."[9]

Interestingly, it is also in a woman's best interest to work toward providing home support. According to research done at Ohio State University College of Medicine, marital quarrels are harder on women than on men. Blood samples taken from ninety newlywed couples after they had a fight showed that women had higher levels of stress hormones. Researchers noted that men tend to withdraw from conflict or tune out. Women, on the other hand, are more likely to be critical or demanding.[10]

I do want to be fair. I have discovered, as a husband of over twenty-five years, that even godly women who love the Lord sometimes have a bad day. At our home my four boys and I have developed a code among the men. We simply say, "Mama has that look in her eye!" I came home one day when we were living in Wake Forest and was met by all four boys at the front door.

"Stop, Daddy, stop. Don't go in the house. There's a problem."
I asked them what the problem was, and in unison they said "It's
Mama." I asked them if she was hurt, and they responded no but
added that she was about to kill one of them. Timothy, my
youngest, quickly interjected, "She's got the look, Dad, and she's
got it big time!"

I slipped into the house and looked into the kitchen where
Charlotte was at work at the sink. Our sink was against the back
wall, and so all I could see was Charlotte from the backside.
However, let me tell you that by the way she was conducting business at that sink, I could tell from the back she had the look.
I quickly moved back outside to the boys, gathered them up in a
male huddle, and said, "Guys, we've all seen Mama, and so here's
Dad's counsel. Every man for himself!" I shared with them that
I had seen this look before and that basically this look said, "Give
me some space for about two hours, and I will be fine." I told the
boys that I was not going to bother her or cross her path for the
next couple of hours. I suggested that they do the same, and
I informed them that if they got in trouble with her that they were
not to call me because I was not coming!

Professor Bob Montgomery at Bond University in Australia
says the formula for a happy, nurturing relationship is simple: five
good times for every bad one. "If everything is basically good most
of the time, a marriage can absorb the shocks and problems that
are part of everyone's life—especially if both [partners] are able to
put out the soothing response of humor when these crises
emerge."[11]

A man needs to believe and experience a home that is his
castle. He needs home support, and the wife is essential to his
receiving it.

You are beautiful as Tirzah, my darling,
  lovely as Jerusalem,
    awe-inspiring as an army with banners.
Turn your eyes away from me,
  for they captivate me.
Your hair is like a flock of goats
  streaming down from Gilead.
Your teeth are like a flock of ewes
  coming up from the washing,
  each one having a twin,
  and not one missing.
Behind your veil,
  your brow is like a slice of pomegranate.
There are 60 queens
  and 80 concubines
  and young women without number.
But my dove, my virtuous one, is unique;
  she is the favorite of her mother,
  perfect to the one who gave her birth.
Women see her and declare her fortunate;
  queens and concubines also, and they sing her
  praises. (6:4–9)

HE NEEDS AN ATTRACTIVE WIFE (VV. 4–9; CF. 7:1–9)

Shulammite has praised Solomon, and now he returns the compliment. Yet as he returns the compliment, we learn something more about a basic need that a man has: the need for his wife to be attractive. Solomon begins by telling his love, his darling, that she was like two of the most beautiful and lovely cities in Palestine, the cities of Tirzah and Jerusalem. In Lamentations

2:15, Jerusalem is called the "the perfection of beauty." So unbelievable was the Shulaumite's beauty that Solomon says it was as
if he were facing an awesome army with its banners in full display. Her beauty threw him off balance. So great is her loveliness
that he is almost overwhelmed. "Turn your eyes away from me,
for they captivate me."

Going back to prior descriptions, he again describes the beauty
of her hair, the brightness of her teeth, and the loveliness of her
temples. His love for her has not diminished, and her beauty is as
radiant as ever. Yet he does not stop here. He adds to his previous
praise. He tells her she has a uniqueness that transcends all others.
In verses 8–9, he says there may be "60 queens and 80 concubines
and young women without number," but none of them compare to
her. Again he refers to her as his dove, and then he adds that she is
his "virtuous one" and utterly "unique." This favorable opinion, he
notes, is also shared by her mother, as well as other women. They,
too, call her blessed, and they also praise her.

A man longs for a woman who is possessed of an inner and
outer beauty. A woman who is beautiful to her husband will cultivate a godly and Christlike spirit in her inner self (cf. 1 Pet.
3:1–5). She understands that being beautiful on the inside will
make her more attractive on the outside.

She is also a woman who keeps herself physically fit with diet
and exercise, and she wears her hair, makeup, and clothes in a way
that her husband finds attractive and tasteful. Her husband is
pleased and proud of her in public but also in private. Men, being
creatures of sight, are not impressed with flannel, sweats, or cot-
ton socks. Indeed, Shulammite understood well the need for
Solomon to have a wife that he could be proud of physically and
spiritually, publicly and privately.

His mouth is sweetness.
He is absolutely desirable.
This is my love, and this my friend,
   young women of Jerusalem. (5:16)

HE NEEDS A BEST FRIEND (V. 16)

In the latter part of 5:16, Shulammite says of Solomon, "This is my love, and this my friend, young women of Jerusalem!" Shulammite was well aware that though a man may not always act like it, he needs his wife to be his best friend. How does a wife go about doing this? She develops mutual interests with her husband. She discovers activities her husband enjoys and seeks to become proficient in them as well. If she learns to enjoy them, then she joins him in them. If she does not enjoy them, she encourages him to consider other things that they can enjoy doing together. She works at becoming her husband's best friend so that he repeatedly associates her with those activities he enjoys the most. Men are good at putting on acts and pretenses. However, I have become more and more convinced with each passing year of my own marriage that a man really does need to have a woman, his wife, who is his best friend.

A word of warning is essential at this point. It is wise for a man to have an inner circle of three or four men who are his confidants and with whom he has great trust. I am also unalterably convinced that no woman should be a part of that circle. It is an unwise and dangerous course of action. But in addition to that, in his innermost circle, there must be only one person, and that one person should be his wife. She should be his closest confidant. She should be his closest companion. She should be his best friend. Experts tell us that many long marriages wither from neglect rather than blow up.

"So many times when couples get involved in careers and parenting their children, they lose that emotional connectedness with each other. It slips away and they don't realize it," says Claudia Arp. "She's into her thing, he's into his thing, then when the kids leave—that reason for staying in the relationship goes, too." "In the past, marriages stayed together because society expected you to stay together," says David Arp. "Now if a marriage stays together, it's because the couple wants to stay together."[12]

A husband and a wife should be lovers. The Song of Songs has made this clear. However, a husband and a wife should also be each other's best friend. The Song of Songs has also made this clear, and it is not surprising that there is usually an intimate link between being great lovers and best friends.

A MAN MUST LOVE HIS WIFE

Men and women are different in many ways. One area in particular is in the area of needs. Women have needs that are significantly different than those of men. How has God put a woman together? What does she need from a man?

My love is . . . notable among ten thousand. (5:10)

SHE NEEDS A SPIRITUAL LEADER (V. 10)

Shulammite says that Solomon is "notable," chief or distinguished "among ten thousand." Her primary focus is on his physical appearance, and yet I am convinced she makes this statement as well because of the godly character that radiates from within. It would be difficult to imagine the Bible commending anyone simply on physical appearance alone. Even here in the Song of Songs, the spiritual character of a man is at least implicitly present. A woman's primary need is that her husband would be a spiritual leader. She longs to follow a man of courage, conviction, commitment, compassion, and character.

A woman longs for a man who can be both steel and velvet. He can be a man's man, and at the same time he can be gentle, tender, and approachable. A good woman is worth her weight in gold. However, a good man is worth twice his weight in gold because there are so few of them. *Time* magazine, February 14, 1994, ran on its cover page the body of a man and the head of a pig. The lead article was entitled, "Are Men Really That Bad?" Men have been beaten up severely over the past several decades, and many men deserve those whippings. However, I sense that a new generation is committed to being the kind of man that honors God and blesses a wife. Such a man will be a spiritual leader in the home. He will take the initiative in cultivating a spiritual environment for the family. He will be a capable and competent student of the Word of God, and he will live out before all a life founded on the Word of God. He'll encourage and enable his wife to become a woman of God, to become more like Jesus, and he will take the lead in training their children in the things of the Lord (cf. Eph. 6:4).

You are beautiful as Tirzah, my darling,
    lovely as Jerusalem,
    awe-inspiring as an army with banners. (6:4)

She Needs Personal Affirmation and Appreciation (v. 4)

Solomon refers to Shulammite as his love, his "darling." He tells her how lovely, beautiful, and awesome she is. In verses 5–9 he details those qualities and attributes that he finds so irresistible. His words would have met her need for affirmation and appreciation. A man who loves a woman will praise her for personal attributes and qualities. He will extol her virtues as a wife, mother, and homemaker. He will also openly commend her in the presence of others as a marvelous mate, friend, lover, and companion. She will feel that to him, no one is more important in this world.

I remember telling men in a conference that one of the ways they show their wife appreciation is by picking up the phone and calling her during the day to see how she is doing. He is not to call to ask what came in the mail or what's for supper! The following night a sweet young lady came up to me to tell me that her husband had obviously listened to what I had said the night before. She informed me that they had been married for a number of years and that her husband had never called her during the workday until today. On this day he called her five times! At first I was proud of the impression I had made on the man, but then a frightening thought entered my mind. I asked the lady, "Well, what did he say in each of those conversations?" Tragically, she informed me that he said not much at all and that each conversation lasted no more than a minute. I began to apologize to her for the fact that things had not worked out so well. She quickly interrupted me, "Oh no, Dr. Akin, it was wonderful. Just the fact that he thought to call means everything. We can work on the words later! However, if he doesn't call, we have nothing to work on."

P'Gail Betton explains that, in part, the popular success Bishop T. D. Jakes enjoys with women is due to the constant way he publicly praises his wife. "I am a divorced mother of a 7-year-old, and I like to see a man who loves his wife."[13]

Charlotte and I had some friends in Dallas who would come over to our home and eat pizza and drink Diet Coke on a regular basis. On one occasion my wife was standing in the kitchen getting some drinks ready. Just sort of spontaneously and without really thinking about it, I said to her, "Charlotte, girl, I do believe you are about the most beautiful thing I have ever seen." She smiled at me and I smiled back.

Then one of my friends, whose name was Cathy, said to me, "Danny, I love it when you say nice things about Charlotte in front of other people, and you do it a lot." I had not really thought about it that much before, and so I turned to Cathy and said, "You mean when John (her husband) says nice things about you in front of other people, it means a lot?" She responded with a twinkle in her eyes, "Hardly anything he does makes me feel more special."

Men, we need to be reminded that words of appreciation and affirmation, in front of other people, speak to one of the deepest needs in the life of our wife.

> *There are 60 queens*
> > *and 80 concubines*
> > *and young women without number.*
> *But my dove, my virtuous one, is unique;*
> > *she is the favorite of her mother,*
> > *perfect to the one who gave her birth.*
> *Women see her and declare her fortunate;*
> > *queens and concubines also, and they sing her praises: . . .*

I came down to the walnut grove
      to see the blossoms of the valley,
      to see if the vines were budding
      and the pomegranates blooming.
Before I knew it,
      my desire put me
      among the chariots of my noble people.

Come back, come back, O Shulammite!
Come back, come back, that we may look at you! (6:8–9, 11–13)

SHE NEEDS PERSONAL AFFECTION AND ROMANCE (vv. 8–9, 11–13)

Romance for a man means sex. He cannot imagine romance without having sex. Romance for a woman can mean lots of things, and sex may or may not be a part of it. Solomon recognizes the need to cultivate an environment of romance, and so he tells Shulammite in 6:8–9 that no one compares to her when it comes to other women. She is his "unique" one (v. 9). All those who see her "declare her fortunate," and they "sing her praises." In verses 11–13, we find her response to the praise that has been showered on her by Solomon. She moves to the garden to see the beauty of it and the fresh evidences of their love. This is depicted by her desire to see whether the "vines were budding and the pomegranates blooming." Even before she was aware of it, her soul had been enraptured, and she was "among the chariots of my noble people." Verse 13 pictures her being swept away, while those who look on her beauty and perfection (at the encouragement of her husband, it should be noted) plead with her to return and not to go away. A woman who responds in this way has had her deepest need for affection and romance met by her husband.

It is crucial that a man learn how to speak to the needs of his wife's heart in the area of romance. He must demonstrate to her both in word and deed that he understands her unique needs and appetites in this area. Most men do not understand romance from the female perspective. Most men would not recognize romance as women understand it if it were to slap us in the face or bite us on the nose.

I became acutely aware of this when I came home one day when we were living in Dallas, and I asked my wife Charlotte, "Honey, do you think I'm romantic?" She yanked her head around so quickly, it is amazing to me that she did not permanently damage her neck. There was a look in her eyes that I had never seen before, but I was certain that I was not going to like what she would say. Being the loving wife that she is, she began by saying, "Let me start by saying that I do love you, and I cannot imagine being married to anybody else but you. You are a good husband and a wonderful father. However, I must tell you that the answer to your question is no. You are not romantic. I doubt that you would recognize it if it slapped you in the face or bit you on the nose."

As you can imagine, my feelings were hurt, and so I responded in typical male fashion, "I've been reading a lot about this stuff lately, and all these books that I have been reading say you need it." She responded by telling me that she did, and so I told her that I might try to begin to give it to her in the near future. I must add at this point, I had no idea exactly how that was going to happen, but I was pleased when she said, "The fact that you're even going to try, I find romantic."

Now I want all of you to know that what I am about to tell you is absolutely the truth with no embellishment. Feel free to look up my wife anytime and have the story verified. It was a Friday night. I snuck up behind Charlotte feeling that it was time to be romantic (you guys know what that means!). I began to rub her back and neck. After just a couple of moments, she turned around and looked at me and said, "Why don't you go on, leave me alone, and quit bothering me." I responded by telling her that I thought that was romantic. She informed me that it was not romantic now, nor would it be romantic later either. I clearly understood what that meant, and so I went off to bed early that night by myself. There was no need in waiting up.

The next morning my wife took a shower. When Charlotte takes a shower, she always loves to put on her body an Avon product called Skin-So-Soft. Those of you who are familiar with it know that it does three things: (1) It smells really good. (2) It will slime your dry skin if it needs it. (3) It also happens to be a wonderful insect repellant. Charlotte pats this on her body and then wipes it off with a towel. Her towel was lying on the bed after she had gotten out of the shower. I walked over and did an unusual thing. I picked up her towel and I smelled it. I turned to Charlotte and I said innocently, "Honey, this towel smells like you."

She responded by saying, "Now that's romantic." I looked at her, stunned at her statement, and I said, "You don't have to make fun of me. I am really trying at this romance thing." She responded by telling me that she really did find my statement romantic, and she walked out of the bedroom. At that point I looked up into heaven and told God there was no hope in this area as far as I could see. I would never be able to understand romance from the female perspective. At that point God was gracious to me, and He gave me insight as to how this romance thing works from the female perspective. I now share it with all my fellow males throughout the world.

Romance is basically a game. It is a specific game. It is a game of "hide-and-go-seek." She hides it and you seek it. If you find it, you will indeed agree that it's good! On the other hand, if you don't find it, you have one of two options. First, you can get nasty, mean, and bent out of shape and just be a miserable old grouch for the rest of your life. I have met a number of men just like that. Or second, you can remind yourself, it's a game. Sometimes I win, and sometimes I lose. But that's the fun of playing the game.

But there's a second part to this game, and this is not fair. However, we dealt long ago with the fact that some things aren't fair; it's just the way they are. Guys, you must understand. What is romantic to your wife, say, on Monday, may not necessarily be romantic on Tuesday. Indeed, women are adept at moving the romance on a regular basis, sometimes even hiding it in places where they can't even find it. When you go searching for romance in the place where it used to be, but now you discover that it is no longer there, don't be surprised if looking over your shoulder is the woman that God gave you, and with her eyes she says something like this, "Yes, my darling. I moved the romance. It's somewhere else now. And I'm going to wait to see if you love me enough to look for it all over again."

Now again, guys, you can get angry, mean, and bent out of shape, or you can remember, it's a game. And games can be fun. Sometimes you win, and sometimes you lose. But it's all a great game. Men, if you will approach romance in this way, not only will you find it fun, but you will also get better at it along the way. Carlin Rubenstein reminds us, "The level of romance in a

relationship is a kind of barometer of love: When romance is
low, couples have sex less often, are less happy about love, and
are more likely to consider divorce."[14]

His mouth is sweetness.
He is absolutely desirable.
This is my love, this my friend,
   young women of Jerusalem. (5:16)

SHE NEEDS INTIMATE CONVERSATION (V. 16)

Shulammite states that Solomon's mouth is sweet and that "he
is absolutely desirable." When one compares this verse with verse
13, it is clear that she has in mind, at least in part, his kisses and
physical expressions of his love. Yet, as we have seen, statements
are often capable of more than one meaning. She is also complimenting him with respect to the words that proceed from his
mouth, declaring that they are sweet.

A woman needs intimate conversation. She needs a husband
who will talk with her at the feeling level (heart to heart). She
needs a man who will listen to her thoughts about the events of
her day with sensitivity, interest, and concern. Daily conversation with her conveys her husband's desire to understand her.
Wise men learn soon after marriage that women are masters of
code language. They say what they mean and expect you to
know what they mean, and the particular words really don't
matter. Unfortunately some men are simply ill prepared and a
little dense at this point, and it often gets them into serious
trouble.

How often it is that a man will come into the house in the
evening, walk into the kitchen, give his wife a kiss on the cheek,

and ask her the question, "Honey, how was your day?" He will receive the response, "Fine." Now if he is listening to the tone in which the word *fine* is delivered, he will pick up that *fine* does not mean "fine," *fine* means "bad." Unfortunately, he isn't listening. He retires to their family room and grabs that male therapy device, the remote control, unaware of what just transpired.

However, about three hours later it hits him. She didn't fix me any supper. Men become amazingly sensitive when they're hungry. And so this starving warrior makes his way to the bedroom where he finds his wife, and he asks a simple question, "Honey, is anything bothering you?"

She simply and curtly responds, "No." Now of course, this *no* means "yes." It also means this: "You weren't interested in finding out three hours ago, and I'm not about to tell you now. Indeed, this world will come to an end before you know what's bothering me."

Now a man could try to blame this whole episode on his wife, but the fact of the matter is, the blame lies at his feet. When he came in and kissed her on the cheek in the kitchen and asked about her day, she screamed loud and clear, "I've had a horrible day. Nothing's gone right. I need you to stay here for a few moments and let me just vent and get some things out of my system." Ten minutes of undivided attention can absolutely revolutionize the way the rest of the evening will go. A man must learn to meet his wife's need for intimate conversation.

> *Who is this who shines like the dawn—*
>   *as beautiful as the moon,*
>   *bright as the sun,*
>   *awe-inspiring as an army with banners? . . .*

Come back, come back, O Shulammite!
Come back, come back, that we may look at you! (6:10, 13)

SHE NEEDS HONESTY AND OPENNESS (VV. 10, 13)

Solomon is utterly transparent and open in his affection and
love for Shulammite. In 6:10 he says that she "shines like the
dawn," is "as beautiful as the moon," as "bright as the sun," as "awe-
inspiring as an army with banners." Nothing is hidden; everything
is out in the open when it comes to his love and affection for her.
A woman needs her husband to be honest and open with her. She
needs a man who will look into her eyes and, in love, tell her what
he is really thinking (Eph. 4:15). He will explain his plans and
actions clearly and completely to her because he regards himself as
responsible for her. He wants her to trust him and feel secure. He
wants her to know how precious she is to him. Growing openness
and honesty will always mark a marriage when a man loves a
woman.

> *What makes the one you love better than another,*
> *   most beautiful of women?*
> *What makes him better than another,*
> *   that you would give us this charge? . . .*

> *Where has your love gone,*
> *   most beautiful of women?*
> *Which way has he turned?*
> *We will seek him with you. . . .*

> *Come back, come back, O Shulammite!*
> *Come back, come back, that we may look at you! (5:9; 6:1, 13)*

SHE NEEDS STABILITY AND SECURITY (5:9; 6:1, 13)

In 5:9, the young women of Jerusalem respond to the loving words of Shulammite in 5:8. They acknowledge that in her view, he is better than any other. In 6:1, the young women of Jerusalem again request of Shulammite the location of her love. It is clear in their mind that she knows where he is and that she is secure and certain in that knowledge. Even when he has "turned aside," she is aware of where he is located. In verse 13 where her friends call for her to return, it is clearly implied that she is in his presence and that he is carrying her away to be with him. He has placed her in his chariot, and they are going away. She is secure in the love of her husband.

A man who loves a woman will firmly shoulder the responsibilities to house, feed, and clothe the family. He will provide and he will protect. He will never forget that he is the security hub of the family for both his wife and his children. She will be aware of his dependability, and as our text indicates, so will others. There will be no doubt as to where his devotion and commitments lie. They are with his wife and his children.

> But my dove, my virtuous one, is unique;
>   she is the favorite of her mother,
>   perfect to the one who gave her birth.
> Women see her and declare her fortunate;
>   queens and concubines also, and they sing her praises. (6:9)

SHE NEEDS FAMILY COMMITMENT (6:9; CF. 8:1–2)

The family is not directly mentioned in the Song of Solomon, and children are notably absent. Yet in 6:9 Solomon makes reference to the fact that "she is the favorite of her mother, perfect to the one who gave her birth." Solomon knew that drawing upon this family imagery would speak to her heart, and it would also impress upon her his interest in the family, and the importance he would place upon it. A woman longs to know that her man puts the family first. Such a man will commit his time and energy to the spiritual, moral, and intellectual development of the entire family, especially the children. For example, he will play with them, he will read the Bible to them, he will engage in sports with them, and he will take them on other exciting and fun-filled outings. Such a man will not play the fool's game of working long hours, trying to get ahead, while his spouse and children languish in neglect. No, a woman needs a man who is committed to the family. She needs a man who puts his wife and children right behind his commitment to the Lord Jesus Christ.

> When 1,500 mall shoppers were asked what they wished
> for most when they blow out their birthday candles, men
> and women gave vastly different answers. The number
> one wish of women was "more time with spouse."
> Among men that wish came in at 27th on the list. (What
> did the guys wish for most often? A lower golf score.)[15]

Bill McCartney, former football coach at the University of Colorado and head of Promise Keepers, says, "When you look into the face of a man's wife, you will see just what he is as a man. Whatever he has invested or withheld from her, is reflected in her countenance."[16]

"An anthropologist once asked a Hopi why so many of his people's songs were about rain. The Hopi replied that it was because water is so scarce and then asked, 'Is that why so many of your songs are about love?'"[17]

When a woman puts her husband where her heart is, she makes it her ambition to meet five basic needs in his life. When a man loves a woman, he makes it a life goal to meet seven basic needs of his wife. When a husband is committed in this way, and when a wife has the same commitment, it is not surprising that both husband and wife have a smile on their faces and joy in their hearts. This is the way God intended it from the beginning. As persons committed to God's plan for marriage, we should settle for and expect nothing less.

Chapter 11

Men Behaving Beautifully

SONG OF SOLOMON 6:13–7:10

Men can be rather peculiar creatures. In the minds of women, often they are downright strange. A good friend of mine by the name of Charles Lowery was for a time a senior pastor in Albuquerque, New Mexico, and today is a wonderful marriage and family conference speaker. Several years ago he tried to help us get a grip on the mind of the male in a column he wrote. I think you'll find this both entertaining and right on target.

Men

A few years ago the Forester Sisters sang a song about men. It went something like this: "They buy you dinner, open your door, other than that what are they good for?" Men. . . . Men do have problems, especially with relationships. We grow up playing baseball, football, king of the hill, and capture the flag. We grew up competing with each other—doing things and fixing things. We don't talk much, especially about our feelings. You might say that deep down, men are real shallow.

A man thinks talk is a four-letter word. He thinks the relationship is going great if he doesn't have to talk. Putting him in a situation where he has to talk makes him very uncomfortable. That's why men go to the bathroom alone, the way God intended it. [As a quick aside, let's face it, women do not honor the sanctity or privacy of the bathroom. But guys, we should have seen it coming. At a public gathering women head for the ladies' rest room like a pack of wolves. A man, on the other hand, is perfectly capable of taking care of business all by himself. In fact guys, think of the utterly repulsive and yucky feeling you get just thinking how you would respond if another man invited you to go to the rest room with him! No worry men, it won't happen in this lifetime!]

A man just has difficulty expressing himself. My daughter will call and I will say only three things: "How's the weather, need any money, here's your mother." A woman can talk on the phone 30 minutes and you say, "Who was that?" She says, "I don't know, she got the wrong number."

Things are simple with a man. Women are complex. They may even be smarter. Think about it. A woman's best friend is diamonds, and man's best friend is a dog. Yes, women are more complex. When a woman is going out, she has to decide if she is going to wear her hair up or down, flats or high heels, slacks or dress, casual or dressy dress, stockings, knee highs or socks, jewelry or no jewelry, lots of makeup or little makeup. A man picks up some clothes, smells them, and if there is no visible dirt he has himself an outfit!

A man makes a fashion statement by turning the brim of his baseball cap backwards. Women dress to express themselves and men dress so they won't be naked. . . .

Of course the bottom line is look at what women carry—a purse. It contains everything she might need. Men carry a wallet. It conveniently contains nothing but money, which means you can buy whatever you need. Simple! But these differences affect many aspects of a relationship.

Let me tell you "simple" doesn't work when dealing with your wife, especially in the area of gifts. If your last gifts have been things like salad shooters, dust-busters, weed whackers, deluxe irons and drywall compound, you are in serious trouble. They work, but they don't work with your wife. . . .

Yes, we're different. That was God's plan. The difference is the dynamic. Together we could be more than we could ever have been apart. That's why God said it wasn't good for man to be alone. I will make him a helper to complete him . . . or was it to finish him off?

Yes, men and women think and act differently. Unfortunately, far too many men both think and act badly. In the fall of 1996, *NBC* introduced a sad, sick comedy called *Men Behaving Badly*. It depicted men as crude, rude lowlifes, scumbag-dogs pure and simple. The Song of Songs, however, has a different take on men. It shows us men who behave beautifully, men behaving as God intended when He created them in His image and saved them through His Son Jesus Christ. What does this man, this husband, look like? Solomon highlights three truths.

Come back, come back, O Shulammite!
Come back, come back, that we may look at you!

Why would you look at the Shulammite,
    as you would at the dance of the two camps?
How beautiful are your sandaled feet,
O princess!
The curves of your thighs are like jewelry,
    the handiwork of a master.
Your navel is a rounded bowl;
    may it never lack mixed wine.
Your waist is a mound of wheat
    surrounded by lilies.
Your breasts are like two fawns,
    twins of a gazelle.
Your neck is like a tower of ivory,
    your eyes like pools in Heshbon
    by the gate of Bath-rabbim.
Your nose is like the tower of Lebanon
    looking toward Damascus.
Your head crowns you like Mt. Carmel,
    the hair of your head like purple cloth—
    a king could be held captive in your tresses.
How beautiful you are and how pleasant,
    O love, with such delights! (6:13–7:6)

HE ADVANCES IN THE PRAISE OF HIS MATE (6:13–7:6)

We have already seen Solomon praise his wife twice for her physical beauty and priceless character (4:1–7; 6:4–9). In each description there is growth in appreciation for her. Each is more personal, intimate, sensual, and developed. A friend of mine heard that I was teaching the Song of Songs over a five-month period and asked, "How can you take that much time? Haven't you found the book to be rather repetitious?" I answered him with a yes and a no. I readily acknowledged the repetition, but quickly pointed out that repetition is often the best teacher. I also pointed out that God obviously thinks (and probably our spouses too) that we cannot say kind and uplifting things too often to our mates. Finally I noted that the repetition we discover is seldom, if ever, identical. There is growth and progress in the love, knowledge, and joy this husband and wife share. Solomon is advancing, growing in the school of praise of his mate. What are some of the particulars we discover?

Praise Her Publicly (v. 13)

Solomon sweeps his wife off her feet and places her in his "royal chariot." He publicly honors her. This display of affection draws the praise of her friends who plead with her to return that they "may look at" her. Four times the imperative "come back" is voiced. But she is gone. She has left all for a man who is so public, in this instance even without words, in his love for his wife. The word *Shulammite* is used only here in the Song. It is actually the feminine form of *Solomon,* literally *Solomoness.* It means "perfect one."[1]

Shulammite is taken aback by the praise she receives and responds with a question: "Why would you look at the Shulammite, as you would at the dance of the two camps?" This latter phrase is unclear, but her question and action are not. They have praised her beauty, and she is appreciative. But there is another whose praise means even more. That person is her husband. His praise has freed her to express herself with unhindered, sensual abandonment. She will now dance nakedly and seductively. This dance is not for many but only for one. It will be a private performance reserved only for her husband. There is power in public praise.

PRAISE HER PHYSICALLY (VV. 1–5)

This is the third and most sensual and detailed physical description by Solomon of his wife. Starting from her dancing feet to a woman's glory (her hair, see 1 Cor. 11:15), Solomon describes physical features of his wife which draw attention to her beauty as a woman. One thing is obvious: she has removed her outer garments and dances in the light clothing of a shepherdess; or, more likely, she dances fully naked, wisely and seductively appealing to the male's heightened sense of sight.[2]

However, let's keep this all in perspective. What constitutes a sensuous and attractive woman is probably a badly misunderstood idea by most. A *USA Today* survey asked men what they first noticed about a woman. Interestingly, the number one answer was the eyes (39%). Second was the smile (25%). Only 14 percent said the first thing they noticed was the body.[3] Different men find different kinds of women attractive. I think Linda Dillow and Lorraine Pintus say it best when they write, "Nothing is as 'sexy' as a woman who gives in to her sensuousness, a woman who enjoys sex and lets her husband know she loves to give and receive pleasure."[4] Going on to quote Lisa Douglass, they add, "Nothing transcends the traditional definitions of beauty like the face and the body of a passionately aroused woman."[5]

PRAISE HER PARTICULARLY (VV. 1–5)

Solomon focuses on ten aspects of his wife's beauty. Though attention is on the physical, certain features also highlight the attractiveness of her personality and character as well.

She dances before him, and so he mentions first her feet. Her "sandals" would have left the top of her feet nearly bare. This would have been alluring and particularly attractive.[6] His reference to her as a "princess" is a symbolic way of praising her noble character, and it testifies to how her husband views and treats her. He honors her as God commands (1 Pet. 3:7). There are no demeaning glances, no rude snapping of the fingers, no harsh words of contempt or criticism. She is a princess, a queenly maiden.

Her thighs are shapely and priceless, the work of a skilled craftsman. The word refers to the upper part of the thigh where the legs begin to come together.[7] Like priceless jewels they are attractive to see and precious to hold.

Verse 2 is badly translated, in my judgment, in virtually every English version. The problem is with the word "navel." It simply does not fit the upward progression or description. The Hebrew word is rare, occurring only three times in the Old Testament (cf. Prov. 3:8; Ezek. 16:4). Here the word almost certainly is a reference to the innermost sexual part of a woman, her vagina (vulva).[8] Solomon's description makes no sense of a navel, but it beautifully expresses the sexual pleasures he continually receives from his wife. Like "a rounded bowl" or goblet it never lacks "mixed wine"; she never runs dry. She is a constant source of intoxicating pleasure and sweetness. The idea of blended or mixed wine could refer to the mingling of male and female fluids in the appropriate part of a woman's body as a result of sexual climax.[9]

Shulammite was an exotic garden (4:12, 16) and an intoxicating drink (7:2) in her lovemaking. Seldom, if ever, was her husband disappointed. She was his dream lover, and amazingly, he wasn't dreaming!

He compares her waist to "a mound of wheat surrounded by lilies." This could refer to her gently curved figure and also to the fact that she was like food to him. She is wheat and wine, food and drink. She nourishes and satisfies him in every way.

He again describes her breasts as "two fawns" (cf. 4:5). They are soft and attractive, enticing him to pet them. Her neck is "a tower of ivory" (cf. 4:4). She is majestic, stately, a confident and dignified lady. Her eyes are beautiful, pure and refreshing (cf. 1:15; 4:1), like the Moabite city of Heshbon (cf. Num. 21:25), a city known for its reservoirs. The location of Bath-rabbim is unknown, though it is possibly the gate in Heshbon that led to the pools. Her "nose is like the tower of Lebanon looking toward Damascus." She is strong in character, and there is a genuine sense in which he draws strength and security from her. He may also be saying, "Her nose complements and sets off her facial beauty."[10]

"Your head crowns you like Mount Carmel," he says (v. 5). The Carmel range was considered to be one of the most beautiful in all of Palestine. She is beautiful and unique, majestic and awesome (cf. Isa. 35:2; Jer. 46:18). Her hair is like purple (or deep red), and her husband is "held captive" by its beauty. He has been ensnared by her; a king has been captured.

PRAISE HER PERSONALLY (V. 6)

Solomon summarizes his praise of his wife by telling her she is beautiful and pleasing, a love with delights. He is specific and personal. Physically she is stunning, and personally she is pleasant. She is his love and lover, and he associates nothing but delight with her. What man would not willingly allow himself to be captured by such a lady?

I think I know something of what Solomon felt. When I was dating Charlotte, a number of my friends playfully remarked, "Danny's been caught in Charlotte's web." I had indeed been trapped and captured by her beauty from head to toe (or toe to head following Solomon here). I'm glad to report, over twenty-five years later, I still haven't escaped! A man who behaves beautifully will advance in the praise of his mate and enjoy all the good things that follow.

> *Your stature is like a palm tree;*
> > *your breasts are its clusters.*
> *I said, "I will climb the palm tree*
> > *and take hold of its fruit.*
> *May your breasts be like the clusters of grapes,*
> > *and the fragrance of your breath like apricots.*
> *Your mouth is like fine wine—*
> > *flowing smoothly for my love*
> > *gliding past my lips and teeth! (7:7–9)*

He Is Aggressive in the Pursuit of His Mate
(vv. 7–9)

Variety is said to be the spice of life, and when it comes to sex, nothing could be more true. An article entitled "Keeping the Romance Alive" pointed out that we should give attention to at least four categories of sexual activity:

The Quickie—quick, fast and a gift from one to the
   other.
Normal—the 20 to 30 minutes of married sex.
Romantic Variety—sex on vacation, in a hotel.
Adventuresome Sex/Cliffhanger Sex—new positions,
   new places.[11]

Solomon is certainly creative and imaginative as he expresses
his desire for Shulammite. He is not dull or boring, nor does he
display a one-track mind. He is always looking for new and fresh
ways to communicate his affection.

EXPRESS A DESIRE FOR HER LOVE (VV. 7–8)

Solomon compares his wife to a stately, swaying palm tree and
her breasts to its clusters. Her breasts are a sweet and tasty fruit
that he finds irresistible. He moves quickly to express his intentions: "I will climb the palm tree and take hold of its fruit."
Solomon has watched his wife dance nakedly before him as long
as he could. His passion is at a fever pitch. He leaves nothing to
chance; he does not assume his wife understands what he is feeling. He tells her and he tells her plainly.

A man should not make assumptions when dealing with a
woman, especially his wife. It can get him into serious trouble. In
our first year of marriage, I made such an assumption. I assumed
a particular object lesson would make the appropriate impression
on my wife, Charlotte. Boy, was I wrong!

We sat down one Saturday evening to eat a sandwich for dinner. As she placed a wonderful sandwich on the table, Charlotte
also put beside it a Tupperware product that had inside of it, if you
used your imagination and a magnifying glass, something that

remotely resembled potato chips. Once these crumbs were placed in your mouth, you could easily have assumed it was a new variety of chewing gum. They were awful.

I turned to Charlotte and said, "Honey, I don't like these. They're too small and stale. I want some big, fresh, crispy, potato chips." She responded, "Sweetheart, when all of these are gone, we can get some more."

That was not the answer I was looking for, and so I said, "But darling, I saw in the pantry on the way in here a brand new bag of fresh, crispy potato chips that has never been opened. I want those!"

Quick as a flash she shot back, "Well, sugar dumpling, when this container is empty, we can get those."

I then did something that a man would only do in his first year of marriage. I stood up, took her Tupperware, and dumped the chips in the floor! I then said, "This one is empty now. You can go and get the others."

It probably won't surprise anyone that she did not go get the other chips, it was rather chilly at our house (and in our bed) for several days, and I learned the danger of assuming my wife would appreciate my creative object lesson.

EXPRESS DELIGHT FROM HER LOVE (VV. 8–9)

Solomon tells Shulammite that he wants her and that he senses she wants him. I wonder how he got that idea?! Her breasts, her breath, and her mouth all are sources of sensual desire and delight. Her breasts are attractive and sweet. Her breath is fragrant like apricots or apples.[12] The deep, sensual kisses of her mouth are intoxicating like "fine wine." Shulammite had earlier described her husband's mouth in this way (1:2). He now returns the

compliment. The environment has been set for a time of meaningful romantic lovemaking.

John Gries is on target when he writes, "Jesus intended
marriage to be happy for you. God expects regular sex in marriage, and sex is a learning process." In his book *Sex 101: Over 350
Creative Ways to Combine Sex, Romance and Affection,* Gries
points out seven essentials for satisfying sex. They include communication, time, patience, experimentation, understanding,
being teachable, and humor. He notes, "Every ingredient is very
important."[13]

> RNS reported that "Family, money and religion are
> even more important to Americans than sex, accord-
> ing to a new survey on attitudes toward sexual
> health." But that does not mean Americans devalue
> sex. Of those surveyed, 82 percent said sexual satisfac
> tion was important or very important. "Loving family
> relationships," received the most votes, with 99 per-
> cent considering it important or very important.
> Financial security was a close second, receiving 98
> percent. Ranked third, religion and spiritual life was
> considered important or very important by 86 per-
> cent. . . . "This survey is a 'snapshot' in time that
> looks at how American adults view issues related to
> sexuality and sexual problems as a whole," said
> Dr. Marianne J. Legato of Columbia University.
> Researchers also found that age did not affect the
> importance people placed on sex. The vast majority
> of respondents, 94 percent—split almost equally
> between men and women—agreed that "enjoyable

sexual relations add to a person's quality of life, even
when they grow older."

Yes, we should expect delight from the love of our mate. And the
good news is that it can get better with each passing year.

Your mouth is like fine wine—
  flowing smoothly for my love
  gliding past my lips and teeth!
I belong to my love,
  and his desire is for me. (7:9–10)

HE ACCEPTS THE PASSION OF HIS MATE (VV. 9–10)

It has been some time since Shulammite has spoken (6:13).
She has been carefully listening and taking in all that her husband
has said. He has gotten the attention of her heart, and again it was
through her ear, through what she heard. Now it is her time to act,
and act she does. What do we discover about the pleasures of passion in a good marriage?

LET THERE BE MUTUAL GIVING (V. 9)

Picking up on the imagery of wine, Shulammite expresses her
desire to satisfy and bring pleasure to her husband. "The wine goes
down smoothly for my beloved [HCSB "love"] moving gently the
lips of sleepers [or "lovers"]."[14] They are making love to each
other, and it is delightful—like fine, intoxicating wine. They
exchange kisses and intimate expressions of love that each finds
satisfying. His goal is to satisfy and please her. Her goal is to satisfy and please him. When there is mutual giving with the goal of

pleasing your mate, the marvelous result will be that both spouses will experience the joy and pleasure God intended for us (cf. 1 Cor. 7:3–4; Phil 2:3–5).

Susan Townsend says we must play fair when making love. This entails:

Flirting (a smile and a look)

Appreciate (and express it)

Intimacy (let you know me)

Risk (have adventuresome sex; talk about new topics;
    keep the spice).[15]

LET THERE BE MUTUAL GRATIFICATION (V. 10)

There have already been refrains or statements of mutual possession (2:16; 6:3). However, this time the statement is different. Rather than read, "I am my lover's and my lover is mine" (6:3), we read, "I belong [am] to my lover, and *his desire is for me.*" This is a strong affirmation of possession and gratification. She delights in the fact that her husband's desire is for her only. What security! What satisfaction! What safety! She is so taken by his love for her she does not need to mention her possession of him. The word *desire* occurs only here and in Genesis 3:16 and 4:7. It speaks of a strong yearning. Solomon, as is true of all men, has an earnest desire for "the loving approval of his wife."[16] She is grateful for his desire for her, and he is grateful for her admiration and respect.

Passion is not an easy thing to keep aflame over a lifetime, but it is an essential thing. What are some strategies we can put into practice to ensure that flame is never extinguished? Let me quickly give you several:

Twelve Ways to Keep Passion Alive in Your Marriage

1. Work at It

A lifetime of love and romance takes effort. Few things in life are as complicated as building and maintaining an intimate, passionate relationship. You need to work on it constantly to get through those trying periods that require extra work.

2. Think as a Team

When making important decisions, such as whether to work overtime or accept a transfer or promotion, ask yourself this question: What will the choice I am making do to the people I love? Try to make the decision that will have the most positive impact on your marriage and your family.

3. Be Protective

Guard and separate your marriage and your family from the rest of the world. This might mean refusing to work on certain days or nights. You might turn down relatives and friends who want more of you than you have the time, energy, or inclination to give. You might even have to say no to your children to protect time with your spouse. (The kids won't suffer if this is done occasionally and not constantly.)

4. Accept That Good and Not Perfect is OK When It Comes to Your Mate

No one is perfect. You married a real person who will make real mistakes. However, never be content with bad. Always aim for great, but settle for good!

5. Share Your Thoughts and Feelings

Unless you consistently communicate, signaling to your partner where you are and getting a recognizable message in return, you will lose each other along the road of life. Create or protect communication-generating rituals. No matter how busy you may be, make time for each other. For example, take a night off each week, go for a walk together every few days, go out to breakfast if you can't have dinner alone, or just sit together for fifteen minutes each evening simply talking, without any other distractions.

6. Manage Anger and Especially Contempt Better

Try to break the cycle in which hostile, cynical, contemptuous attitudes fuel unpleasant emotions, leading to negative behaviors that stress each other out and create more tension. Recognize that anger signals frustration of some underlying need, and try to figure out what that need might be. Avoid igniting feelings of anger with the judgment that you are being mistreated. Watch your nonverbal signals, such as the tone of your voice, your hand and arm gestures, facial expressions and body movements. Remain seated, don't stand or march around the room. Deal with one issue at a time. Don't let your anger about one thing lead you into showering the other with a cascade of issues. If different topics surface during your conflict, flag them to address later. Try to notice subtle signs that anger or irritation is building. If you are harboring these feelings, express them before they build too much and lead to an angry outburst. Keep focused on the problem, not persons. Don't turn a fairly manageable problem into a catastrophe. Emphasize where you agree.

7. Declare Your Devotion to Each Other Again and Again

True long-range intimacy requires repeated affirmations of commitment to your partner. Remember: love is in what you say and in how you act. Buy flowers. Do the dishes and take out the trash without being asked. Give an unsolicited back rub. Committed couples protect the boundaries around their relationship. Share secrets with each other more than with any circle of friends and relatives.

8. Give Each Other Permission to Change

Pay attention. If you aren't learning something new about each other every week or two, you simply aren't observing closely enough. You are focusing on other things, not one another. Bored couples fail to update how they view each other. They act as though the roles they assigned and assumed early in the relationship will remain forever the same. Remain constantly in touch with each other's dreams, fears, goals, disappointments, hopes, regrets, wishes, and fantasies. People continue to trust those who know them best and who accept them.

9. Have Fun Together

Human beings usually fall in love with the ones who make them laugh, who make them feel good on the

inside. They stay in love with those who make them feel
safe enough to come out to play. Keep delight a priority.
Put your creative energy into making yourselves joyful
and producing a relationship that regularly feels like
recess.

10. Make Yourself Trustworthy

People come to trust the ones who affirm them. They
learn to distrust those who act as if a relationship were
a continual competition over who is right and who
gets their way. Always act as if each of you has
thoughts, impressions, and preferences that make
sense, even if your opinions or needs differ. Realize
your partner's perceptions will always contain some
truth, and validate that truth before adding your perspectives to the discussion.

11. Forgive and Forget

Don't be too hard on each other. If your passion and
love are to survive, you must learn how to forgive. You
and your partner regularly need to wipe the slate clean
so that anger doesn't build and resentment fester.
Holding on to hurts and hostility will block real intimacy. It will only assure that no matter how hard you
work at it, your relationship will not grow. Do what
you can to heal the wounds in a relationship, even if
you did not cause them. Be compassionate about the
fact that neither of you intended to hurt the other as
you set out on this journey.

12. Cherish and Applaud

One of the most fundamental ingredients in the intimacy formula is cherishing each other. You need to celebrate each other's presence. If you don't give your partner admiration, applause, appreciation, acknowledgment, the benefit of the doubt, encouragement, and the message that you are happy to be there with your beloved now, where else will your partner receive those gifts? Be generous. Be gracious. One of the most painful mistakes a couple can make is the failure to notice and acknowledge their partner's heroics. These small acts of unselfishness include taking out the trash, doing the laundry, mowing the lawn, driving the carpool, preparing the taxes, keeping track of birthdays, calling the repairman, and cleaning the bathroom, as well as hundreds of other routine labors. People are amazingly resilient if they work and receive appreciation in the process. Make a concerted effort to notice daily acts of heroism by your loved ones. (Source unknown)

Most of us are familiar with the "virtuous woman" of Proverbs 31. She is most certainly a worthy model for all women to emulate. However, you might not be as well informed of the "noble man" of Proverbs 32! Now, if you know your Bible, you will quickly point out, "There is no Proverbs 32 in the Bible." But several years ago a fine student at Southern Seminary in Louisville, Kentucky, wrote something of a modern-day proverb that beautifully expresses what it means for a man to "flesh out" the biblical command to love his wife just as Jesus Christ loved the church and gave Himself [in sacrificial death] for her (Eph. 5:25). Thank you, Michael Jones, for challenging all husbands everywhere to behave beautifully.

Proverbs 32
The Husband of Noble Character
A husband of noble character who can find? He is worth more than winning the Publisher's Clearinghouse Sweepstakes.

His wife has full confidence in him and lacks nothing of importance.

He brings her good, not harm, all the days of her life.

He works hard to provide for his family. Getting up early he helps get the kids ready for school, then dashes off to work.

With his shoulder to the grindstone, he works with energy and vigor, as one who is working for the Lord. And while busy he always finds time to call his wife during the day just to say, "I love you."

He promptly comes home from work and immediately pitches in with the chores, helping the children with their homework, or with making dinner. While hot dogs and baked beans are his specialty, he doesn't fear heating up a TV dinner or even making a meat loaf. He does this with such ease that all are amazed and in awe.

When his wife prepares a meal, he always eats with gusto and, when finished, never forgets to smile and tell her how great it was. Of course, he is always the first to volunteer to do the dishes or at least to volunteer the children to complete the task!

All in all he is a joy to have in the kitchen.

As a father there is no equal on the face of the earth. No matter how exhausted from work or other responsibilities, he always takes time for his children.

Whether it's making funny faces at the baby, tickling the small child, wrestling or playing with an older child, or making pained and disbelieving expressions at his teenager, he is always there for them.

He is a whiz at math, science, spelling, geography, Spanish, and any other subject his children are studying at school.

And if he should be totally ignorant of the subject at hand, he skillfully hides his ignorance by sending the children to mother.

He can fix any problem from a scraped knee to loose bicycle chains, from interpreting rules for a kickball game to refereeing sparring matches between his kids.

More importantly, he is also the spiritual leader in the family. He always takes the family to church. He shows his children, by life and example, what it means to love the Lord Jesus and be a Christian.

He teaches his children how to pray and the importance of knowing and loving God. He often rises early to pray for his wife and children, and he reads from his Bible at night before falling off to sleep.

He disciplines his children with loving firmness, never yelling or with humiliating words. He is always more interested in teaching a lesson and building character than in simply punishing.

During the day he meditates on God's Word and on how to live it. He shows Christ in all his dealings with others and is considered a valuable employee by his bosses. His coworkers respect his hard work, his integrity, and his kindness.

He always shows his wife the utmost respect, even opening the door for her. He is always quick with a word of encouragement and is constantly telling her how beautiful she is, even when she isn't wearing any makeup.

A day seldom passes that he doesn't tell her of his love for her. Praise for her is always on his lips.

Anniversaries and birthdays are never forgotten, and gifts and flowers are often given "just because."

And he even makes superhuman efforts to be nice when her family is visiting.

He is full of compassion for the pain of others and willingly helps those in need. Whether it's changing a stranger's flat tire, helping with a friend's home improvement project, or feeding the poor at the local soup kitchen, he is the first to volunteer.

He is not afraid to shed a tear with a friend in pain or to be rowdy in laughter at another's good joke.

He loves life and lives it with passion.

His children, while not always calling him "blessed," have no doubts about his great love for them. His wife also calls him many things, among them, "the best," and she thanks God for him.

Many men do many great things, but he surpasses them all.

Flattery is deceptive and good looks, like hair, are fleeting; but a man who fears the Lord is to be praised. Give him the reward he has earned, and let his deeds bring him praise.

Michael M. Jones
Louisville, Kentucky 1996

Chapter 12

A Wonder of a Woman

THE SONG OF SONGS 7:10–8:4

I recently came across some counsel that we men would like to pass on to the ladies that, at least in our judgment, would go a long way in helping you be just the right mate. I call it "25 Essentials for a Fantastic Female."

1. Learn to work the toilet seat. If it's up, put it down. We need it up, you need it down. You don't hear us complaining about you leaving it down.
2. If you won't dress like the Victoria's Secret girls, don't expect us to act like Don Juan or Romeo guys.
3. Don't cut your hair. Ever. Long hair is always more attractive than short hair. One of the big reasons guys fear getting married is that married women always cut their hair, and by then you're stuck with her.
4. Birthdays, Valentine's Day, and anniversaries are not quests to see if we can find the perfect present yet again!
5. If you ask a question you don't want an answer to, expect an answer you don't want to hear.

6. Sometimes we're not thinking about you. Just learn to live with it. Don't ask what we're thinking about unless you are prepared to discuss such topics as March Madness, the shotgun formation, and the stupidity of the "prevent defense."
7. Saturday equals sports. It's like the full moon or the changing of the tides. Let it be.
8. Shopping is not a sport, and no, we're never going to think of it that way.
9. When we have to go somewhere, absolutely anything you want to wear is fine.
10. You have enough clothes.
11. You have too many shoes.
12. Crying is definitely blackmail.
13. Ask for what you want. Let's be clear on this one: Subtle hints don't work. Strong hints don't work. Really obvious hints don't work. Just say it!
14. We don't know what day it is. We never will. Mark anniversaries on the calendar.
15. Yes and no are perfectly acceptable answers to almost every question.
16. Come to us with a problem only if you want help solving it. That's what we do.
17. A headache that lasts for seventeen months is a problem. See a doctor.
18. If something we said could be interpreted two ways, and one of the ways makes you mad or sad, we meant the other one.
19. You can either tell us to do something or tell us how to do something but not both.
20. Whenever possible, please say whatever you have to say during commercials.

21. All men see in only sixteen colors. Peach is a fruit, not a color.
22. It if itches, it will be scratched.
23. If we ask what's wrong and you say "nothing," we will act like nothing's wrong. We know you're lying, but it's just not worth the pain.
24. Anything we said six months ago is inadmissible in an argument today. All comments become null and void after seven days.
25. Most guys own three pairs of shoes. What makes you think we'd be any good at choosing which pair, out of thirty, would look good with your dress?

The ladies may not be impressed with this list from the men. That is understandable. But what if I could give you God's perspective on a fabulous female, a picture of His wonder woman? Would you be interested? I believe such a woman is portrayed in Song of Songs 7:10–8:4. She is not characterized by twenty-five particulars but rather by three overarching attributes that any man would find attractive and irresistible.

I belong to my love,
   and his desire is for me.

Come, my love,
   let's go to the field;
   let's spend the night among the henna blossoms.
Let's go early to the vineyards;
   let's see if the vine has budded,
   if the blossom has opened,
   if the pomegranates are in bloom.
There I will give you my love.

The mandrakes give off a fragrance,
    and at our doors is every delicacy—
    new as well as old.
I have treasured them up for you, my love. (7:10–13)

SHE DELIVERS PERSONAL INVITATIONS FOR LOVE (vv. 10–13)

Solomon, at least at this point in his life, is a one-woman kind of man. Shulammite is a one-man kind of woman. His attention is on her, and her affection is set on him. Kind words of praise and affirmation from her husband have set Shulammite free to respond sensually to her husband. She extends an invitation for a romantic getaway. What are its components?

BE SPECIFIC (V. 10)

Shulammite says, "I belong to my love," "I am my beloved's" (NKJV), "I belong to my lover" (NIV). She belongs to him and no other. He is the only man in her life. The danger of infidelity is not on her radar screen, and she wisely avoids its snares.

The warning signs of infidelity are not difficult to spot. We simply need to be on the lookout. Nine in particular stand out.

Nine Warning Signs of Infidelity
1. The feeling of "going through the marriage motions."
2. Inventing excuses to visit someone of the opposite sex.
3. Increasing male-female contacts in normal environments (e.g.: work, choir, recreation).

4. Being preoccupied with thoughts about another person (something only you and God will know).

5. Exchanging of gifts with a "friend" of the opposite sex.

6. Making daily/weekly contact with someone by phone.

7. Putting yourself in situations where a friend or employee "might" become more.

8. Having to touch, embrace, or glance at a person of the opposite sex.

9. Spending time alone with anyone of the opposite sex.

A wise husband and a wise wife will covenant never to be alone with a person of the opposite sex other than their spouse. Such a commitment is a sure safeguard against adultery and a pledge of the specific and particular nature of one's love and devotion for his/her mate.

Be Secure (v. 10)

Shulammite can also say of her husband, "And his desire is for me." Solomon has eyes for only one woman, and that woman is his wife. This is how it should be for all men, that our desire is only for one lady—our wife. A wife who is secure in her relationship with her husband is released to love him without holding anything back. She does not fear that her love will be prostituted or abused. In an article entitled "New Rules for a Happy Marriage," Sue Ellin Browder gives us seven tips that can help build security in a happy relationship.

1.   Love your differences.

2.   Sweat the small stuff.

3.   Laugh.

4.   Put your heads together.

5.   Stay connected.

6.   Take a leap of faith.

7.   Relive beautiful moments.[1]

BE SPONTANEOUS (VV. 11–12)

For the first time in the Song, Shulammite takes the initiative in requesting a time for romance and lovemaking with her husband. She knows that sex that takes place only at home can run the risk of becoming routine. Vacations and special getaways often enhance and rekindle passion in marriage. She invites him to leave the city and its grind and to go away with her to the country for a time where they can be alone together. Four times she says, "Let's go."

Spring is a universal symbol of love and romance, and the signs should be everywhere in a marriage. There should be a freshness and a sense of anticipation to love. Getting away, if only for a brief time, can invigorate and energize a relationship. Shulammite knows sexual problems can slip into a relationship if it is not properly cared for. As a woman, she is aware of the role she must play to keep their sex life on a high plain. Ginny Graves outlines seven essentials that a woman must give attention to in order to keep the flames of romance raging:

1.   **Adjust Your Hormones.** Sex and hormones are inextricably linked . . . hormonal upheaval can strike in a woman's mid-to-late forties, before

menopause sets in. "In some women, when
levels of sex hormones decrease around
menopause, so does sex drive," says Barbara
Sherwin, professor of psychology and obstetrics/
gynecology at McGill University in Montreal.

2. **Sleep Well.** "Sleep deprivation is an underrated
    cause of decreased sex drive," says Kathleen
    Blindt Segraves, associate professor of psychia-
    try at Case Western Reserve University School
    of Medicine in Cleveland, Ohio. The treatment
    is easy and inexpensive: seven to nine hours of
    shut-eye a night.

3. **Exercise Wisely.** Most of the news about exer-
    cise and sex is good. According to one study,
    aerobic exercise (an hour a day) has been
    shown to increase sexual frequency and
    responsiveness in men, and researchers
    assume it gives women the same libidinal zing.
    Extreme exercise, however, may cause a back-
    lash. . . . To reap exercise benefits, be sure to
    maintain a moderate workout schedule,
    increase the intensity of your regimen gradu-
    ally, and consume enough calories to preserve
    a healthy level of body fat.

4. **Beat Depression.** "Depression has a constella-
    tion of symptoms, including loss of interest in
    sex," says Xavier Amador, a New York City
    psychologist.

5. **Watch Those Anti-Depressants.** "One of the
    great ironies of anti-depressants is that they

can cause sexual dysfunction," says Dr. Andrew
Leuchter, director of the Division of Adult
Psychiatry at U.C.L.A.

6. **Manage Stress.** "Even everyday stressors correlate
    with reduced sexual desire in men and women,"
    says J. Gayle Beck, professor of psychology at the
    State University of New York at Buffalo. "Men are
    more likely to put their feelings aside in the inter-
    est of having sex, whereas women will choose not
    to have a sexual encounter," she says. When stress
    builds up, people become too distracted to focus
    on giving and receiving sexual pleasure. "It's no
    coincidence," says Beck, "that a lot of couples have
    great sex when they're on vacation." If you suspect
    that stress is causing low libido, find time to
    decompress by taking a bath or a long walk early
    in the evening.

7. **Communicate.**[2]

BE SENSUAL (vv. 12–13)

Budding vines, blossoms opening, pomegranates, and especially mandrakes were all considered aphrodisiacs. Some
referred to the mandrake as the "love apple."[3] In the midst of
these outdoor delicacies, Shulammite says, "There I will give you
my love." Not just in the country but outside under the sun,
moon, and stars we will find a place just for the two of us and
make passionate love.

Barbara O'Chester of Austin, Texas, speaks to thousands
of women every year about marriage, sex, and romance. She

recognizes that some women struggle in the area of romance and experiencing their own sexual pleasure. Why? She notes ten reasons:

1. Ignorance	6. Passivity
2. Resentment	7. Hormonal
3. Guilt	8. Overweight
4. Physical Problems (Illnesses)	9. Fatigue
5. Fear	10. Lack of Time

The Song of Songs provides some real assistance in overcoming a number of these. Fatigued? Take a vacation. Lack of time? Get away. Do as verse 13 directs: At the door of your mate, find "every delicacy." Lay aside your inhibitions and let your imagination run wild. Find "all manner" of pleasant fruit. Some will be old (it is good every time without fail), and some should be new (different, previously unexplored). Shulammite says she has all of this stored up for her husband, and a wise man will certainly say, "Let's enjoy." And guys, not only will it be fun; it is also good for you. The British Heart Foundation released a report that says men who make love three or four times a week are protecting themselves against heart attacks and strokes. Men who have three to four orgasms a week cut in half the risk of having a major heart attack or stroke over the next ten years. Indeed, good sex is as good an exercise as jogging or squash.[4] While the research did not look at the impact of sexual activity on women's long-term health, I'm sure the benefits are even better for them!

> *If only I could treat you like my brother,*
> *one who nursed at my mother's breasts,*
> *I would find you in public and kiss you,*
> *and no one would scorn me.*

I would lead you, I would take you,
    to the house of my mother who taught me.
I would give you spiced wine to drink,
    and the juice of my pomegranates. (8:1–2)

SHE DECLARES THROUGH PUBLIC AFFECTION HER LOVE (vv. 1–2)

These two verses sound strange to our modern Western ears, but they would have spoken beautifully and affectionately to the heart of Solomon. Indeed it is the case that kind, loving words are welcomed anytime and anywhere. They are crucial to keeping us well connected. We all might be well served to take a little advice from the family dog at this point.

"Fido may do a better job of greeting your spouse when he or she comes home than you do," says William Doherty, director of the Marriage and Family Therapy program at the University of Minnesota in St. Paul. The family dog is loyal, enthusiastic and totally focused on the greeting ritual. But your opening words to your spouse just might be a question about having left the garage door open or remembering to pay a bill. And that attitude makes a difference. Small "couple rituals"—such as a loving greeting—add up in the long run. They help maintain connection between partners and "are the glue we need to help us cling together in times of stress and in seasons of despair," Doherty says. The absence of such intimate rituals may indicate that a marriage is drifting along on "automatic pilot."[5]

Nothing was on autopilot in this marriage. Shulammite made no assumptions, and she left nothing to chance. She wanted her husband and the world to know how she felt. What do we learn from her?

SHOW YOUR LOYALTY TO EACH OTHER (V. 1)

Shulammite says she wishes Solomon was her brother so she could shower him publicly with affectionate kisses. In the Ancient Near East, it was considered appropriate only for near relatives to engage in such public displays of love and affection. "The freedom to kiss in public would not apply to her husband."[6] Shulammite regrets this. She wants all to know how she feels about her husband. She will not overturn accepted social expectations and suffer scorn and ridicule. She will not be despised. Her actions may have to be curtailed for the moment, but her words trumpet a message that is music to the ears and heart of her husband.

Pawing one another in public is still in bad taste. Gracious and genuine tokens of our love, loyalty, and affection are always welcomed. They will be well received by our mate, and they will provide testimony to others of our devotion to each other.

A lonely heart, even in marriage, is often a sick heart—and in more ways than one. In an article entitled "Lonely Hearts Often Have Sick Hearts," Ronald Kotulak notes:

> Loneliness is bad for the heart in more ways than one, according to new research that shows the physiological toll of psychological isolation. But the research, conducted by a team from the University of Chicago and Ohio State University also suggests a remedy: Just saying hello or being nice in other small ways can help prevent

heart attacks among the lonely. The study found that
being lonely is a major risk factor of heart disease, as bad
as a high-fat diet, high blood pressure, obesity, smoking or
physical inactivity. Loneliness tends to raise blood pressure
and disrupt sleep, both of which put people at greater risk
of heart trouble. Population experts long have known that
lonely people tend to be sicker and die younger, but they
didn't know why. Women with few social contacts and
who feel isolated, for instance, have a greater risk of dying
of cancer. Married cancer patients have better outcomes
than unmarried cancer patients. But loneliness is not just
being alone. It involves feelings of isolations, of discon-
nectedness and of not belonging, each of which can occur
when a person is in a crowd or alone. Lonely people per-
ceive their world as less reinforcing and more threatening.
They may not have a romantic partner or close friends.[7]

Demonstrate in clear and unambiguous ways your love and loyalty to each other. Remember: it's good for the heart.

STRENGTHEN YOUR DESIRE FOR EACH OTHER (V. 2)

Shulammite begins to play with her husband. She assumes the
role of an older sister and tells him how she would relate to him.
She would lead him and take him into the house of her mother.
The word for *lead* refers to "a superior leading an inferior: a general, his army; a king, his captain; a shepherd, his sheep. . . . She
would lead her younger brother to their common home."[8]
Shulammite notes it was at home that she received instruction
from her mother. In the context she must mean instruction about
matters of sexual intimacy and love. This is a valuable lesson,

especially for those of us who are parents. "The art of preparing for love is best learned at home."[9]

Dads and moms must take charge at appropriate times and in appropriate ways in teaching their children about the birds and the bees. They cannot leave this vital task in the hands of the schools. They dare not entrust it to locker room or girlfriend talk. Dads must instruct their sons, and mothers must guide their daughters. This does not mean dads have no part in training their daughters or moms in assisting their sons, but sexual identity often will play a role in who takes the lead with whom.

Shulammite informs Solomon of some things she learned from her mother. "Spiced wine," special wine, would be on their lover's menu as well as the juice of the pomegranate. "An ancient Egyptian love poem identifies a wife's breasts with the fruit of the pomegranate."[10] Duane Garrett points out that the reference to her "mother's house" could easily be a euphemism for the intimate sexual parts of the woman.[11] That the overtones of her words are sensual and erotic are undeniable. The joy of lovemaking they share does not wane but grows more intensive and creative as their marriage progresses. And much of the credit goes to Shulammite.

In an article entitled, "When He's Not in the Mood," Michele Weiner-Davis provides some helpful advice to build and maintain sexual passion in marriage, especially if things are on a downturn at the present.

Men
1. Get a complete medical check-up.
2. Check carefully any medications you are taking.
3. Check your hormone levels, especially your testosterone.

4. Measure any signs of depression.

5. Evaluate frustration or resentment over unre-
    solved relational issues.

6. Educate yourself about the sexual aspects of
    marriage and the needs and desires of a
    woman.

Women

1. Take action to rekindle the fire. Don't be
    passive.

2. Spice things up with a new location, new posi-
    tions, lingerie, candles; cast your inhibitions to
    the wind.

3. Quit nagging—it is men's #1 complaint about
    their wives and is a certain turn-off.

4. Engage in self-care.

5. Be supportive.

6. Give him space.[12]

His left hand is under my head,
   and his right hand embraces me.
Young women of Jerusalem, I charge you:
   do not stir up or awaken love
   until the appropriate time. (8:3–4)

SHE DEMONSTRATES HER LOVE THROUGH PRIVATE CONSUMMATION (VV. 3–4)

An article in *Maxim,* a popular men's magazine said,
"Monogamy is man's greatest challenge. It takes unshakable

commitment, intense emotional maturity, a will of steel in the face of overwhelming temptation. In other words, it ain't gonna happen."[13] I don't believe this. In fact, I reject such an argument with every fiber of my being. When a man loves a woman like this Song teaches and when a woman puts her man where her heart is as this Song instructs, the passion, commitment, and devotion they enjoy will produce a glue that will hold them together until death parts them. Solomon and Shulammite again are engaged in the act of lovemaking, but the focus this time is a bit different. It is also instructive.

TENDERNESS IS ENSURING (V. 3)

"His left hand is under my head, and his right hand embraces me." Solomon gently and tenderly is holding and caressing his wife. Perhaps they have just finished making love, and they rest in each other's arms in the afterglow of the moment. He does not leap out of bed and run downstairs for a snack. He doesn't grab the remote control to get a sports update from ESPN. She doesn't slip out of bed to make a quick phone call, nor does she rush out of the room to attack unfinished chores. They simply lie there loving and holding each other. They are tender in their affections, and tenderness speaks to the heart and soul of one's mate.

In an article entitled "Nourishing Your Love," Marie Pierson advises women in how to touch a man's heart. Here are her six suggestions:

1. Show him admiration and appreciation.
2. Nurture his friendship.
3. Lower your expectations. (You married a real person!)

4.   Watch your priorities. (Is he #1 after Jesus?!)
5.   Enhance your love life.
6.   Be forgiving. (Even as God in Christ has for-
      given you. Eph. 4:32)[14]

TIMING IS IMPORTANT (V. 4)

For the third time (cf. 2:7; 3:5) the importance of the proper
time for lovemaking is addressed. Obviously God believes timing
is important. First, it is the right time for lovemaking only in marriage between a man and a woman. Second, within marriage, timing and sensitivity to the needs and feelings of our mate is crucial
as we build affection and romance in our marriage.

Some popular pundits say the modern Christian advice concerning sex dates to 1973 and a book by a woman, Marabel
Morgan's *The Total Woman.* Actually, advice for Christians concerning sex goes all the way back to the Book of Genesis when
prior to the fall, Adam and Eve "were both naked and . . . not
ashamed" (Gen. 2:25 NASB). The climax of God's counsel we find
in the Song of Songs. Here we discover that our God says sex and
romance are good in marriage. Indeed they are essential. It is
encouraging to see that more and more Christians "see sex more
as a gift to be enjoyed within marriage than as an evil to be
endured or avoided,"[15] and that, "an orthodox view of romance,
courtship and sexuality" may be the best road to sexual satisfaction. Solomon worked at doing his part. In these verses we have
seen Shulammite doing her part. Why hasn't it always been this
way? After all, God's plan for the Christian bedroom has never
changed. It is a good thing. It is a great thing. Yes, it is a God thing.

Chapter 13

Love That Lasts a Lifetime

THE SONG OF SONGS 8:5–14

Love is wonderful. It can also be dangerous. I heard about the teenage boy who went into the drugstore and asked the druggist for a one-pound, a three-pound, and a five-pound box of candy. When the druggist asked him why he wanted three different boxes, he said, "Tonight I have a date with the most beautiful girl in our school. She is drop-dead gorgeous. I've been in love with her for years, and I finally worked up enough nerve to ask her out, and she said yes. Unfortunately our first date is having dinner with her parents. But after dinner, we're going to go outside and sit in their porch swing, and I have really high hopes about that. If before the night is out I get to hold her hand, I'm going to give her that one-pound box of candy as a gift. But sir I must tell you, my goals for this night are much higher. If she lets me put my arm around her and hold her real tight, I'm going to give her that three-pound box. But, if before our date ends, she lets me give her a big wet kiss right on her mouth, I'll give her that five-pound box of candy as a gift."

The druggist sold him his three boxes of candy, and the young man went home. In preparation for the date, he did all the things a man, young or old, married or unmarried, should do before a date. He took a shower and used shampoo and soap. He brushed his teeth and used mouthwash. He put on deodorant and cologne, as well as nice clean clothes.

After arriving at his date's home and visiting for a while in the family room, they went into the dining room for dinner. The father asked the young man to say the blessing, and boy did he. He prayed fifteen minutes for the meal! When he finished, his date looked at him and said, "I had no idea you were so spiritual." The young man looked back at her and said, "Yes, and I had no idea your daddy was the druggist either!"

Yes, love is wonderful. Love is dangerous. Love can also be confusing. It is often the case that we get love confused with infatuation, and the mistake can be disastrous. I came across an article that contrasts the two. I think you'll find it is right on target.

Love or Infatuation

Infatuation leaps into bloom. Love usually takes root and grows one day at a time. Infatuation is accompanied by a sense of uncertainty. You are stimulated and thrilled but not really happy. You are miserable when he is absent. You can't wait until you see her again. Love begins with a feeling of security. You are warm with a sense of his nearness, even when he is away. Miles do not separate you. You want her near. But near or far, you know she is yours and you can wait.

Infatuation says, "We must get married right away. I can't risk losing him." Love says, "Don't rush into anything. You are sure of one another. You can plan your future with confidence."

Infatuation has an element of sexual excitement. If you are honest, you will discover it is difficult to enjoy one another unless you will know it will end in intimacy. Love is the maturation of friendship. You must be friends before you can be lovers.

Infatuation lacks confidence. When he's away, you wonder if he's with another girl. When she is away, you wonder if she is with another guy. Sometimes you even check. Love means trust. You may fall into infatuation, but you never fall in love. Infatuation might lead you to do things for which you might be sorry, but love never will.

Love lifts you up. It makes you look up. It makes you think up. It makes you a better person than you were before.

Song of Solomon thinks love is important, so important in fact that it constitutes the final theme of the book. Twelve different aspects of love are addressed. Love truly is, according to God's Word, "a many splendored thing."

Who is this coming up from the wilderness,
leaning on the one she loves? (v. 5)

LOVE IS PUBLIC (V. 5)

It appears that Solomon and Shulammite are riding again in the royal chariot in full public display. She reclines relaxed and secure "leaning on the one she loves." The phrase "coming up from the wilderness could be echoing the theme of Israel's forty years of wandering in the wilderness before entering the promised land.

This couple has passed through those wilderness periods in their marriage and safely arrived on the other side. "The wilderness" also could convey the idea of cursedness (see Jer. 22:6; Joel 2:3). Their love relationship is a redeemed relationship through God's grace. The effects of the fall and the Genesis curse (Gen. 3:16ff) have been reversed and the disharmony that sin brings into a relationship overcome. This is what God can do when He is Lord of our marriage. As Frederica Matthews-Green says, "Women need men to call us up toward the highest moral principles; [men] need [women] to call them down to the warmth of human love and respect for gentler sensibilities. . . . It's clear that we need each other. You would almost think someone planned it that way."[1] The love that Solomon and Shulammite enjoy is something all the world should see and learn from.

> *Under the apricot tree I awakened you.*
> *There your mother conceived you;*
>> *there she conceived and gave you birth. (v. 5b)*

LOVE IS PRIVATE (V. 5)

Shulammite again initiates lovemaking (the "I" is feminine). Apparently they have left the chariot and are now alone. Three times in the Song we have been told not to awaken love until the time is right (2:7; 3:5; 8:4). The time is now right according to Shulammite. The apricot (or apple) tree was often associated with sexual activity and romance in the ancient world. "It was the sweetheart tree of the ancient world."[2]

The last part of verse 5 is an example of Hebrew parallelism. "There your mother conceived you; there she conceived and gave you birth." Garrett points out:

She calls her beloved an apple tree in 2:3 and thus the
figure of his mother being "under the apple tree"
means that his mother was with his father. Similarly,
the place where his mother conceived and gave birth to
him refers to the female parts. . . . The woman means
she and he are now participating in the same act by
which the man himself was given life.[3]

As we have seen throughout this book, sex is an important
and significant part of a good marriage and with good reason.
Married sex is more satisfying than recreational sex or cohabiting
sex for both men and women.[4] Indeed Linda Waite, coauthor of
The Case for Marriage, says, "Just being married seems to improve
women's satisfaction with sex . . . while marriage works for men
sexually by giving them an active and varied sex life."[5] However,
we do need to be fair and honest about this area. Sometimes, as we
have seen in this book, the sparks don't fly, and the flame is barely
at pilot light. Why? The reasons vary. Barbara DeAngelis, author
of *How to Make Love All the Time,* warns us of five traps we must
avoid.

Trap #1: Waiting until late at night to have sex
Trap #2: Falling prey to statistics paranoia
Trap #3: Stalling until you're in the mood for sex
Trap #4: Getting completely out of the habit
Trap #5: Using fatigue as a cover-up for other problems

Barbara quickly counters, however, with a fourfold strategy to
turn things around.

Solution #1: Plan time for sex

Solution #2: Plan decompression time after work

Solution #3: Give yourself permission to have
    "quickies"

Solution #4: Stop trying to fill a sexual quota; enjoy the
    sex you do have[6]

This is sound counsel, and coupled with the advice we receive in the Song, we can confidently and expectantly look forward to those private times for love.

Set me as a seal on your heart. (v. 6)

LOVE IS PERSONAL (V. 6)

Shulammite asks her husband to set her as a seal upon his heart. A person's seal was extremely important and personal. In part, it indicated ownership and was placed upon a person's most valued possessions. This wife wants to know she is her husband's most personal and valuable possession. She wants to be a seal but a seal placed in a particular location, upon his heart. In the world of Solomon, it was customary to wear a signet ring or cylinder seal on a cord or necklace around the neck. For Solomon to love his wife in such a way that she felt near his heart would speak of unbreakable devotion and commitment.

How can we demonstrate this personal component of love to our mates so that they know they are indeed a precious seal upon our heart? Perhaps a little marital intimacy test might provide some assistance. Answer the following ten questions and use a basic four-point scale like we do in school.

Marital Intimacy Test

(Answer: 4–often, 3–often enough, 2–not enough,
1–rarely, or 0–never for each.)

1. How often do you show affection for each
    other? _____
2. How often do you laugh at each other's jokes?
    _____
3. How often do you say something nice to each
    other? _____
4. How often do you compliment your partner in
    front of others? _____
5. How often do you enjoy sexual intimacy? _____
6. How often are you playful with each other? _____
7. How often do you look each other in the eyes
    while talking? _____
8. How often do you give each other a little sur-
    prise? _____
9. How often do you say "please?" _____
10. How often do you say "I'm sorry?" _____

Add up your points and divide by 10. You will get your
score per a 4.0 scale. You will also get some insight into
the personal aspect of your love.

As a seal on your arm. (v. 6)

LOVE IS PROTECTIVE (V. 6)

Shulammite also desires to be a permanent possession upon her husband's arm. The arm speaks of strength and security. This woman understands that in true love there is always a feeling of safety. There is rest in the relationship we enjoy with our mate.

True love does have a protective attitude. You desire to shield the one you love from any harm, from any injury, from any damage, from anything that will in any way be detrimental. Food for thought: One of the most "lethal weapons" in a relationship is the little chipping at one another with sarcastic barbs. This is especially hurtful when done in front of others. You develop a person by magnifying his strengths, never his weaknesses. Take pride in each other. Learn to protect each other.

One key to this protective component of love is knowledge. The better we know our mates the better equipped we are to give them protective love. So let's ask the question, "How well do you really know your spouse?" A deep and genuine knowledge leads to friendship, and being best friends is crucial to a satisfying marriage. So let's take another little quiz.

Answer the following either True or False:
1. I can name my partner's best friends.
2. I know what stresses my partner currently faces.
3. I know the names of those who have been irritating my partner lately.
4. I know some of my partner's life dreams.
5. I am very familiar with my partner's spiritual beliefs.

6.   I can outline my partner's basic philosophy of life.

7.   I can list the relatives my partner likes least.

8.   I know my partner's favorite music.

9.   I can list my partner's favorite three movies.

10. I know the most stressful thing that happened to my partner in childhood.

11. I can list my partner's major aspirations.

12. I know what my partner would do if he/she suddenly received ten million dollars.

13. I can relate in detail my first impressions of my partner.

14. I ask my partner about his/her world periodically.

15. I feel my partner knows me well.

Scoring: If you answered true to more than half, this is an area of strength in your marriage. You know what makes your partner tick. If not, you have some work to do. Take time to learn more about your spouse to make your relationship stronger.[7]

For love is as strong as death;
 ardent love is as unrelenting as Sheol. (v. 6)

LOVE IS POSSESSIVE (V. 6)

Love is said to be "as strong as death; ardent love . . . as unrelenting as Sheol" (or the grave). Love is both universal and unavoidable, just like death. This is the only occurrence of the word *strong* in the Song. The word means "an irresistible assailant or an immovable defender."[8] When love calls, its siren sound is so compelling you cannot resist it. Love "never releases those whom it has once seized."[9]

"Ardent love" is a strong emotional attachment to a particular person or thing. This type of love is possessive and exclusive. It swallows down men and women once it has laid hold of them just as possessively and certainly as does the grave.[10] "In godly love a righteous jealousy is as hard or inevitable as the grave."[11] It will not let go.

When I played football our coaches tried to motivate us with a saying that went something like this: "When the going gets tough, the tough get going." That may well be true. However, of one thing I am certain: "When the going gets tough, love keeps going." It refuses to quit, drop out of the race, throw in the towel, or let go of the object of its affection. As Paul says in his beautiful chapter on love in 1 Corinthians 13:7–8, "Love bears all things . . . endures all things. Love never fails."

In true love there is a feeling of belongingness. The person in love always thinks of himself in relationship to the other person, and it's a beautiful way to love. What is he doing? What is she doing? What is he thinking? What is she feeling? Real love is possessive. It is not, as one skeptic on marriage said, "two singletons living under the same roof."[12]

> Love's flames are fiery flames—
> the fiercest of all. (v. 6)

LOVE IS POWERFUL (V. 6)

Love "burns like blazing fire, like a mighty flame" (NIV). The emphasis is on the power and intensity of the fire. It is interesting to point out that the last syllable of "flames" in the Hebrew text could refer to the divine name of the Lord, "Yahweh." The Jerusalem Bible, American Standard Version (1901) and the NIV (marginal reading) all take it this way. If this is correct, God Himself is seen as the source of this love. The power of its nature would, therefore, only be strengthened. The love God kindles in a marriage over which He is Lord is such a fervent and fiery flame that nothing on earth can extinguish it or put it out. Like a raging forest fire, it burns with such an intensity that no one can control it. This is a passionate love, a red-hot flame.

In his book *Sustaining Love*, David Augsburger notes that marriages move through stages. In fact, he speaks of four marriages in a marriage. For example, in stage 1 we dream, in stage 2 we become disillusioned, in stage 3 we discover, and in stage 4 we experience depth. It is this fourth stage for which we should aspire as it is here that we find the true power and promises of love. In addition to depth, we also find true communication, celebration, acceptance, intimacy, interdependency, and hope. Here we are not "blinded" by love; we are "bound together" by love. We create "sacred times" for each other because the power of love has made us soul mates.

Mighty waters cannot extinguish love;
rivers cannot sweep it away. (v. 7)

LOVE IS PERSEVERING (V. 7)

And You Wonder Why It Didn't Last
She married him because he was such a "strong man."
She divorced him because he was such a "dominating male."

He married her because she was so "fragile and petite."
He divorced her because she was so "weak and help-
    less."

She married him because "he knows how to provide a
    good living."
She divorced him because "all he thinks about is busi-
    ness."

He married her because "she reminds me of my
mother."
He divorced her because "she's getting more like her
mother every day."

She married him because he was "happy and romantic."
She divorced him because he was "shiftless and fun-loving."

He married her because she was "steady and sensible."
He divorced her because she was "boring and dull."

She married him because he was "the life of the party."
She divorced him because "he never wants to come
    home from a party."

Marriage is meant to last, and so is love. It is not for a season
but for a lifetime. Solomon teaches us that the love God gives cannot be stopped; its flame cannot be put out. Though "mighty
waters" or even floods come against it, it will not be extinguished.
It will persevere. "The tenacious staying power of love is set
against these tides and perennial rivers which are unable to wash
love away or put out its sparks."[13]

Bob and Gloria Cooper have been married for over fifty years.

They are just a regular kind of couple. Concerning their own marriage, Bob said, "This marriage is a covenant. It isn't anything you walk away from. You just make it work."[14] Indeed love may mean staying even when you want to leave. David Sanford provides valuable counsel in this context when he writes:

> Why should you stay in your marriage if you really want to divorce? Quite possibly reasons for staying will include 1) honoring your spouse, 2) respecting your children's needs, 3) caring about family and friends, and 4) property, support and separate housing. You will probably not be asked to consider that you should stay in your marriage in order to learn how to love, despite the fact that this reason for honoring the marriage commitment is one of the most compelling of all. You remember love. If you were typical of most people love was one of your prime reasons for getting married. You were much in love back then. You had a partner who loved you and, you believed, would go on loving you into the future. That was your expectation in getting married. Of course, you loved your partner, too. Doing so was part of being in love and probably was a pleasure, rather than a difficulty. What a shock to learn that loving is primarily not what you receive but what you do—and do even when boredom, resentment, or a hunger for novelty tells you that life can be better somewhere else.[15]

True love, God's kind of love, is persevering.

> *If a man were to give all his wealth for love,*
> *it would be utterly scorned. (v. 7)*

LOVE IS PRICELESS (V. 7)

True love cannot be bought. It has no price tag. It is not for sale. If a person were to give all that he owned to buy love, he would be despised and scorned, subjected to public ridicule and mockery. "By its very nature love must be given. Sex can be bought, love must be given."[16]

What are some clear and concrete ways in which we can give the priceless gift of love to our mate? Joanna Weaver helps us out with her "25 Ways to Love Your Lover."

25 Ways to Love Your Lover

1. List the top 10 reasons "I'm the most fortunate husband/wife in the world." Read them aloud to your spouse.
2. Surprise your mate by doing one of his or her chores. When asked why, give a smooch and say, "Because you are worth it."
3. Don't just show—tell! Say, "I love you."
4. Communicate your plans to each other. On Sunday night go over your schedules for the coming week.
5. Use the T.H.I.N.K. method to determine whether an issue needs to be brought up. Is it true? helpful? important? necessary? kind?
6. Plan an appreciation celebration for your mate, complete with his or her favorite meal.
7. Look at your schedule. Make time with your spouse a weekly priority.

8. Bring back those dating days. After picking up the sitter, walk back outside and knock on the door with flowers in your hand.

9. Don't turn on the TV until after dinnertime, if at all. Wait for a conversation to break out.

10. Pray together. Thank God for your mate, then pray for his or her special needs.

11. On your spouse's birthday send your in-laws a thank-you card.

12. Set boundaries in outside relationships. Don't let anyone take away too much of the time you spend with your spouse.

13. Are you seeing eye to eye? Experts have found the deeper the love, the more frequent the eye contact.

14. Pull out old love letters, taking turns reading and reminiscing.

15. Take turns reading from the Bible each night.

16. Stretch out birthdays with special activities, fun surprises, and a whole lot of hoopla.

17. Be a student of your spouse. Learn what he likes. Learn what she needs.

18. Treat your wife like a lady. Open doors and hold chairs.

19. Throw away fighting words like "you never" and "you should." Use healing words like "I'm sorry" and "you may be right."

20. Make church attendance a joyful priority.

21. Instead of making a joke at your spouse's expense, give a sincere compliment.

22. Create traditions as a couple by budgeting
     money for special times together.

23. Be affectionate. Back rubs and tender hand-
     holding communicate love.

24. Choose your battles carefully.

25. Be a person of integrity. Give your spouse no
     reason to doubt your word or question your
     commitment.

Our sister is young;
   she has no breasts.
What will we do for our sister
   on the day she is spoken for?
If she is a wall,
   we will build a silver parapet on it.
If she is a door,
   we will enclose it with cedar planks. (vv. 8–9)

LOVE IS PURE (VV. 8–9)

Verses 8–12 probably should be understood as a flashback to
Shulammite's youth and initial meeting of Solomon. She grew up
in a family where her brothers had been hard on her (1:6), but
they were also protective. They watched over her and gave attention to her moral development and maturity. Even when she was
"young" and had "no breasts," they kept an eye out for her as they
considered the time when she would give herself to a man in marriage. "If she is a wall" speaks of moral purity and unavailability. If
she demonstrates such character, they will honor her as a tower of
silver. She would be given freedom and responsibility. On the

other hand, "if she is a door," indicating moral vulnerability and weakness, they will enclose her and board her up in order to protect her. If she is reckless and irresponsible in her behavior, they will of necessity restrict her freedom and opportunities for sexual misbehavior and foolishness.

Shulammite's family was wise in their guidance of this young lady. Unfortunately, far too few families provide this much needed guidance in our day. The fallout has been tragic indeed. In an article entitled "Modern Women Get No Respect," Dr. Laura Schlessinger addresses the moral cesspool into which too many women have fallen. She writes:

> Once again we are confronted by feminist outrage at "vicious male behavior" without even a passing nod to the kinds of behavior "sexually liberated women" exhibit. Why shouldn't males in the audience shout at performers such as Sheryl Crow to bare her breasts? Madonna has done it. There are women in Los Angeles and other major cities who go to events to have their breasts signed and who flash their breasts at other drivers on the road. There are scads and scads—legions— of skuzzy, skanky women. Sexy fun is the new norm in America, but I guess that depends on what side of the breast one is on. I know for a fact that people who don't think sexual degradation and license are fun or funny are considered the villains in this country's unfolding immorality play. There is little reason left for society to respect women as it once did. Women get knocked up. They don't marry. They have abortions. They go to bars. They get knocked up again. Major

movie stars proudly get knocked up out of wedlock.
Television stars contribute to our attitudes about
women. Watch prime-time television: How many
women behave with dignity? Where is the feminist outcry about these portrayals, hour after hour, night after
night? . . . How is it that the feminists still don't get it?
They once believed that if women were free to drop
their drawers as often as men, something wonderful
would happen. How did they miss that sexually transmitted disease, abortions, out-of-wedlock births, lack
of respect, and increased vulnerability and exposure to
violence also were going to be part of this package?
I hold no respect for crude male animals. But the male
gender isn't the only one that knows how to oink. As a
general rule, women in our society do not behave in
ways that engender respect. There is a huge population
out there that thinks that's just fine and is ready to
excoriate women who behave in more traditional
female ways. The guys, especially, endorse "the equality
of scuzz." It sure gets them off the hook and releases
them from all responsibility. They can count on
women to abort the results of indiscriminate sex or to
raise the illegitimate offspring all by themselves. I said
a few paragraphs back that we are "almost at the end"
of the sexual revolution. There's one group left for sexual liberation to conquer: our children. The campaign,
tragically, is well under way.[17]

It is indeed the case that the price paid in the loss of female
virtue is not merely a private matter for individual women. The

cost runs much higher and infects the very fabric of the family and the health of the culture. In 1842 Catherine Beecher, the sister of Harriet Beecher Stowe, wrote a book entitled *A Treatise on Domestic Economy for the Use of Young Ladies at Home, and at School*. In it she wrote:

> The formation of the moral and intellectual character of the young is committed mainly to the female hand. The mother forms the character of the future man; the sister bends the fibres that are hereafter to be the forest tree; the wife sways the heart, whose energies may turn for good or for evil the destinies of a nation. Let the women of a country be made virtuous and intelligent, and the men will certainly be the same. The proper education of a man decides the welfare of an individual; but educate a woman, and the interest of the whole family are secured.[18]

I am a wall
  and my breasts like towers.
So in his eyes I have become
  like one who finds peace. (v. 10)

LOVE IS PEACEFUL (V. 10)

Shulammite provides a personal word concerning her chaste moral disposition and value to her husband. She had kept herself morally pure for her husband. She was a virgin when they married. Further, she is now a vibrant, sensual, mature woman of God whose breasts are like towers. When the time came for marriage, she was ready in every way, and her husband reaped the benefits. The text says in his eyes she brought "contentment" or "peace." The Hebrew word is *shalom*. It means wholeness, completeness, and wellness in every part of life. Shulammite made him complete. She was the "helper suitable just for him" (Gen. 2:20). In her presence he was set at ease. He found peace and favor, pleasure and rejuvenation.

> In a recent survey when asked whether they considered their spouse the only person they could have ever married, a surprising 58% answered yes. And, knowing what they now know about their spouse, 89% said they would marry him or her again. 63.8% kiss their spouse more than once a day, 25% once a day and only 3.8% once a month or less. Does marriage get better over time? For 91% of the respondents the answer is yes! Responses include: "It deepens the partnership"; "You grow closer, respect each other, understand differences, feel comfortable together."[19]

And 99 percent said they expected to stay married to their current spouse. All the marriage news isn't bad, is it?

> Solomon owned a vineyard in Baal-hamon.
>   He leased the vineyard to tenants.
> Each was to bring for his fruit
>   a thousand pieces of silver.
> I have my own vineyard.
> The thousand are for you, Solomon,
>   but 200 for those who guard its fruits. (vv. 11–12)

LOVE IS PRIVILEGED (VV. 11–12)

The exact meaning of these verses is vague at best. It seems that the main point is a contrast between Solomon's right to administer his possessions as he chooses (v. 11) and Shulammite's right to give herself as she determines (v. 12). "Solomon had a vineyard at Baal-hamon" (location unknown). "Tenants" oversaw it, and they were to grow enough from the vineyard to produce a thousand pieces of silver. In return they would receive two hundred pieces of silver. This constitutes a five to one profit for Solomon, and this is within his rights as the land belongs to him and he has entered into a mutually agreeable contract with the tenants of the vineyard.

Shulammite also has her own vineyard. It is herself, her body to be specific (cf. 1:6). She belongs to no one, and therefore she has the right and privilege to give herself and her love to whom she chooses. Solomon's vineyard is a possession and impersonal. Her vineyard is a person and thus intimately personal. Gladly, freely, and willingly she has given herself to Solomon to be his wife. Solomon may have thousands of possessions, but she came as a gift.

True love involves a responsiveness to the "total self" of the one loved. You do not fall in love with a body. You fall in love with a person. Indeed it is better stated: "You *grow* in love with a person." In a proper love relationship, you enrich the totality of the other person's life. Furthermore, in true love there is not only a feeling of pleasure but also of reverence. Do you ever look at your wife or your husband and think, *God gave her to me? God hand-tooled him for me?* And true love has a quality of self-giving. God so loved the world that He gave His Son (John 3:16). Many people are in love only with themselves. It has been well said that the smallest package in all the world is the person who is all wrapped up with himself. But in true love a person thinks more of the happiness of others than he does of himself.[20]

You who dwell in the gardens—
  companions are listening for your voice—
  let me hear you!
Hurry to me, my love,
  and be like a gazelle
  or like a young stag
  on the mountains of spices. (vv. 13–14)

LOVE IS PARTICULAR (VV. 13–14)

An English teacher was explaining to his students the concept of gender association in the English language. He stated how hurricanes at one time were given only feminine names and how ships and planes were usually referred to as she. One of the students raised his hand and asked, "What gender is a computer?"

The teacher wasn't certain which it was, so he divided the class into two groups, males in one, females in the other, and asked them to decide if a computer should be masculine or feminine. Both groups were asked to give four reasons for their recommendation.

The group of women concluded that computers should be referred to in the male gender because:

1. In order to get their attention, you have to turn them on.
2. They have a lot of data but are still clueless.

3. They are supposed to help you solve problems, but half the time they are the problem.

4. As soon as you commit to one, you realize that, if you had waited a little longer, you could have gotten a better model.

The men, on the other hand, decided that computers should definitely be referred to in the female gender because:

1. No one but their Creator understands their internal logic.

2. The native language they use to communicate with other computers is incomprehensible to everyone else.

3. Even your smallest mistakes are stored in long-term memory for later retrieval.

4. As soon as you make a commitment to one, you find yourself spending half your paycheck on accessories for it

We have arrived at the end of our Song and the last two verses. Appropriately both the husband and the wife speak, and not surprisingly, the woman gets the last word! Shulammite is in the gardens, she who herself is a garden (cf. 4:12ff). She is a source of perpetual life, joy, excitement, and pleasure to her husband. Friends or companions listen carefully for the voice of this unique and gifted lady. Solomon, however, wants to hear her. His request is exclusive and particular. Others may long to hear her and see her (cf. 6:13), but she is his, and his alone.

He asks her to call out to him. She is not a possession but a person. She is not a slave but a partner. The love she gives is freely given. She responds by inviting him again to go away with her, and she tells him to hurry! She tells him to be free in his sensual feelings for her "like a gazelle or young stag." She invites him to "the mountains of spices," a reference no doubt to her breasts and the pleasures he will find there. Only her lover, her beloved, is welcomed there, and he is always welcomed. They have been married for some time, but the passion and intensity of their love has not waned. This is God's intention. This is God's plan.

The following list of questions can help you analyze your feelings about a possible love relationship. There are no right or wrong answers. Indicate your answer to each question by circling the *Yes, No,* or the *?.* Use the question mark only when you are certain that you cannot answer yes or no. The inventory will be more helpful if both you and your fiancé take it and then discuss it.

Love or Infatuation—Which?

Yes No ?   1. Have the two of you ever worked through a definite disagreement or conflict of interest to the complete satisfaction of both?

Yes No ?   2. Do the two of you progress in your conversations to new views and ideas?

Yes No ?   3. Do you find yourself storing up experiences and ideas to share with your friend?

Yes No ?   4. Are there certain things about your friend that you plan to reform after you are married?

Yes No ?   5. Do you find yourself organizing your plans around this person?

Yes No ?   6. Are you proud to have other persons for whom you have a high regard to meet your friend?

Yes No ?   7. Does the presence or influence of your friend stir intellectual activity or provide inspiration for you?

Yes No ?   8. Are the two of you in agreement on your feelings toward and the handling of children?

Yes No ?   9. Would you have full confidence in trusting your friend in the presence of another attractive person of your sex for an evening?

Yes No ?   10. Do you at times feel uncertain, uneasy, or possessed in your relationship?

Yes No ?   11. When outside trouble develops, does it tend to pull you closer together rather than further apart?

Yes No ?   12. Have you established sexual standards by open discussion, and cooperatively, so that each feels satisfied with the decision reached?

Yes No ?   13. Do you enjoy each other's company when you are together for an evening with no specific activities planned?

Yes No ?   14. Do you ever wonder if s/he is sincere in what s/he tells you?

Yes No ?   15. Do you feel pangs of jealousy when someone else of your sex pays attention to your friend?

Yes No ?   16. Do you find generally that you like the same people?

Yes No ?   17. Are there certain things you need to avoid saying or doing lest there be hurt feelings?

Yes No ?   18. Can you mention specific things or characteristics about your friend that you like?

Yes No ?   19. Do you like his/her outlook on life and the values that s/he holds?

Yes No ?   20. Have you come to understand each other mainly through talking or through experiences you have had together?

Our Marriage Covenant

Recently I came across a spoof on marriage on *The Onion* Web site. Unfortunately there is probably more truth in it than we want to admit.

Darling. We've known each other for more than a year now. During that time, we've shared so much—our hopes, our dreams, our fears. I know when I met you I wasn't thinking of starting up a serious relationship, but my admiration and respect for you quickly blossomed into love. You're my best friend and my confidant, and I can't imagine spending the better part of the next decade without you

I know I've been vague about taking "the next step," but all that has changed. Your patience, loyalty, and love have made me see the world in an entirely new light. It's a place where true love can exist. So I ask you, Julie Bramhall . . . Will you spend the next six to ten years with me?

I realize it's sudden. We just moved in together three months ago, and I'm still looking for a better-paying job. But when I look into your eyes, I see all the things I never used to want. A big wedding. Kids. A house with a white picket fence that I'll have to move out of in about seven years when you discover I'm sleeping with my secretary. I never thought I'd say this to anyone, but you're the only one I want to wake up next to for the rest of my thirties.

I remember telling you early in our relationship that I never wanted to get married. But, sometimes, I stay awake after you've fallen asleep and just look at you and stroke your hair. I can't believe what a lucky man I am. When the moonlight hits your delicate features just right, I see an angel. An angel who will turn cold and indifferent to me in five years because of festering resentment over my drinking. But if I could only capture how you look on film during those moments, I swear we could make a million dollars. God, you're so beautiful at this stage of your life.

Did you know that most of my friends are amazed that a woman of your caliber would even be going out with me, much less be interested in marrying me? They're always talking about how smart, funny, and drop-dead gorgeous you are. I have no choice but to agree. When I take a step back and look at things, there's no reason someone so luminous should be interested in a guy like me. Of course, I always point out to them that your looks will be pretty well faded by 2008. But when I think how stunning you are now, I can only shake my head in disbelief.

Marriage is a big step to make, I know. But when I think of all the memories we've shared together, it makes me want a medium amount more. Do you remember that time we stumbled onto the bridge in Georgia overlooking a moonlit river, and we just held each other close, watching the waves gently lap on the shore? What about all the Sundays we lay in bed together until early afternoon? I cherish these memories, and I want to share more until our relationship is reduced to screaming fights, endless hours of legal battles, and an attempt on your part to stab me with a potato peeler.

If you asked me two years ago if I was ever going to want kids, I would have looked at you like you were crazy. But sometimes, when I'm walking with you hand in hand, I imagine us pushing a stroller. And I like that image. I see us with two kids, a boy and a girl. That would be perfect. They could hold each other up after I'm gone.

I really think you'd make an incredible mother, Julie. And I think you'll eventually make a great single mother, too. You've got that inner strength.

You don't have to answer right away if you don't want to. It's a big decision and I wouldn't want you to take it lightly. Think it over. Talk to your friends and family. I already asked your father for your hand in marriage, and he gave his blessing. But before you answer, you should know that I truly do love you and want to spend nearly a decade with you. Without you, my life is incomplete. At least, until I meet our daughter's dance instructor.

So, please, Julie Bramhall . . . Say you'll grow early middle-aged with me.[1]

Pathetic! Yet the theme is catching on. Fox Television certainly bought into this perspective on marriage. At the beginning of 2001 they debuted a show entitled *I Want a Divorce*. It was a show in which "sparring couples will answer questions about each other for cash prizes and the family property. . . . To find contestants for the game show, Fox has set up a telephone number for couples who wish to compete; a voice encourages callers to go on the show that can turn your divorce into a good thing!"[2]

As we have seen in our study, divorce is really never a good thing for anyone. Pain and heartbreak are always left in its wake. We have looked at the Creator's thoughts on marriage and sex, and we have gleaned some great advice that can help us enjoy marriage not to early middle-age but for life. I truly believe we can. As we close, I want to ask, "Do you?"

A good friend of mine by the name of Dennis Rainey leads a wonderful organization committed to helping marriages and families. It is called FamilyLife Ministries. Several years ago Dennis began to challenge married couples to sign a marriage covenant as a testimony of their commitment to their marriage for life. The result has been nothing short of phenomenal. With his permission I have enclosed here at the end of the book a copy of that marriage covenant and a place for both the husband and wife to sign. If you contact Dennis at FamilyLife Ministries, they will be glad to get you a beautiful copy of the covenant suitable for framing. Simply call 1-800-FL-TODAY or visit their website at www.familylife.com. But now that we have reached the end of our journey, why don't the two of you drop to your knees in prayer and ask God to bless your marriage. Acknowledge your need for Him to be the Lord of your home. Then together, pen your names to the covenant as a declaration to God, each other, and the world that the two of you are in this for life. God will honor you, and together you will discover that this commitment will be a bond that will ensure that you make it, and make it well, to the end. God knows best. Trust Him and see if you don't agree!

OUR MARRIAGE COVENANT

Believing that God, in His wisdom and providence, has established marriage as a covenant relationship, a sacred and lifelong promise, reflecting our unconditional love for each other and believing that God intends for the marriage covenant to reflect His promise never to leave us or forsake us, we, the undersigned, do hereby reaffirm our solemn pledge to fulfill our marriage vows. Furthermore, we pledge to exalt the sacred nature and permanence of the marriage covenant by calling others to honor and fulfill their marriage vows.

In the presence of God and these witnesses, and by a holy covenant, I,

_____

Husband's Name

Joyfully receive you as God's perfect gift for me, to have and to hold from this day forward, for better, for worse, for richer, for poorer, in sickness and in health, to love you, to honor you, to cherish you and protect you, forsaking all others as long as we both shall live.

_____

Husband's Signature

In the presence of God and these witnesses, and by a holy covenant, I,

_____

Wife's Name

Joyfully receive you as God's perfect gift for me, to have and to hold from this day forward, for better, for worse, for richer, for poorer, in sickness and in health, to love you, to honor you, to cherish you and protect you, forsaking all others as long as we both shall live.

_____

Wife's Signature

Witnessed this day, _____

_____

Witness   Witness

Unless the LORD builds a house,
its builders labor over it in vain. (Ps. 127:1)

Endnotes

INTRODUCTION

1. Marilyn Elias, "Marriage Makes for a Good State of Mind," *USA Today,* 14 August 2000.

2. Michael J. McManus, "How to 'Build Children' Rather than 'Build Jails,'" *The Washington Times,* 4 August 2000.

3. Katherine Kersten, "We Should Work to Save Kids from Divorce," *The Minneapolis Star Tribune,* 26 July 2000.

CHAPTER 1

1. Philip D. Harvey, "Divorce for the Best," *Washington Post,* 11 August 2000.

2. James Dobson citing Cheryl Wetzstein, "Researchers See Marriage as a Weakening Institution," *The Washington Times,* 28 October 1999, A2.

3. Matt Ridley, "Will We Still Need to Have Sex?" *Time,* 8 November 1999, 66.

4. Lyndsey Griffiths, "Brave New World," *Toronto Star,* 4 November 1999.

5. The Mishnah is the oral tradition of Judaism which most scholars believe was put into writing in the third century A.D.

6. *Marriage Partnership,* Fall 1998, 10.

7. We are aware of Solomon's own tragic experiment with polygamy as recorded in 1 Kings 11:3. Many scholars believe that in the Song, Solomon is describing the ideal relationship between one man and one woman, as he lamentably knew it should have been.

8. Cited in *Entertainment Today,* 2 January 1997.

9. Tom Gedhill, *The Message of the Song of Songs* (Downers Grove: IVP, 1994), 104.

10. G. Lloyd Carr, *The Song of Solomon,* TOTC (Downers Grove: IVP, 1984), 78.

11. Duane Garrett, *Proverbs, Ecclesiastes, Song of Solomon,* NAC (Nashville: Broadman, 1993), 387.

12. Gedhill, 105.

13. Shirley Barnes, "Keeping It Together," *Seattle Tribune,* 2 August 1998.

CHAPTER 2

1. Gary Smalley and John Trent, *The Gift of the Blessing* (Nashville: Thomas Nelson, 1993).

2. Gedhill, *The Message of the Song of Songs,* 113.

3. Steve Stephens, "37 Things to Say to Your Spouse," in *Stories for the Heart,* compiled by Alice Gray (Sisters, Oreg.: Multnomah, 1996), 177–78.

4. Gedhill, 66.

5. Carr, *The Song of Solomon,* 84–85.

6. Ibid.

7. S. Craig Glickman, *A Song for Lovers* (Downers Grove: Inter Varsity Press, 1976), 37.

8. Norman Bales, *All About Families Newsletter,* 7-26-2000.

9. Tommy Nelson, *The Book of Romance* (Nashville: Nelson, 1998), 26.

CHAPTER 3

1. Patrick Rizzo, "For GenX, Sex Rules," Reuters News Service, June 6, 2000.

2. Stephens, "27 Things Not to Say to Your Spouse," in *Stories for the Heart*, 175–76.

3. Carr, *The Song of Solomon*, 86.

4. Ibid.

5. John G. Snaith, *Song of Songs*, NCBC (Grand Rapids: Eerdmans, 1993), 25.

6. Paige Patterson, *Song of Solomon* (Chicago: Moody, 1986), 45.

7. Ibid.

8. Some students of Scripture believe these verses are a reference to oral sexual pleasure and activity.

9. Carr, 91.

10. Carr, 93.

11. Garrett, *Proverbs, Ecclesiastes, Song of Solomon*, 392–93.

CHAPTER 4

1. Dorthy Rosby, *First for Women*, 23 February 1998, 114.

2. *South China Post*, 25 April 2000.

3. "Spouses Browse Infidelity Online," *USA Today*, 7 June 1999.

4. Gary Chapman, *Toward a Growing Marriage* (Chicago: Moody Press, 1996).

5. Ibid.

6. Richard Leigh and Layng Martine, Jr., "The Greatest Man I Never Knew." used by permission Layng Martine, Jr. Songs (EMI)

and EMI April Music Inc./Lion-Hearted Music (ASCAP) (all rights for Lion-Hearted Music conrolled and administered by EMI April Music Inc.).

7. Erma Bombeck, *Family—the Ties That Bind . . . and Gag!* (New York: McGraw-Hill, 1992).

8. Dale Hanson Bourke, "It Will Change Your Life," *Everyday Miracles* (Nashville: Broadman & Holman Publishers, 1999), 5–8.

9. TK

CHAPTER 5

1. Karen S. Peterson, "Sweet Nothings Help Marriages Stick," *USA Today,* 30 March 2000.

2. Othmar Keel, The Song of Songs, trans. Fredrick J. Gaiser (Minneapolis: Fortress, 1986, 1994), 107.

3. Glickman, *A Song for Lovers,* 47–48.

4. Snaith, *Song of Songs,* 41.

5. *Psychology Today,* July-August 2000, 10.

6. H. Norman Wright, "The 8-Cow Wife," *Marriage Magazine,* May/June 2000.

CHAPTER 6

1. Patricia Donovan, "A Prescription of Sexually Transmitted Diseases," *Issues in Science and Technology* (1993), 9:4, 40.

2. Joe S. McIlhaney, "Improve Nation: Boost Marriage," *Knight Ridder / Tribune News Service,* 29 September 2000.

3. Robert T. Michael, John H. Gagnon, and Edward O. Lauman, *Sex in America: A Definitive Survey* (Boston: Little, Brown & Co., 1994), 124.

4. McIlhaney, "Improve Nation."

5. Michael and others, *Sex in America,* 125.

6. Jan E. Stets, "The Link Between Past and Present Intimate Relationship," *Journal of Family Issues,* 1993, pp. 114, 251.

7. Michael D. Newcomb and P. M. Bentler, "Assessment of Personality and Demographic Aspects of Cohabitation and Marital Success," *Journal of Personality Assessment,* 44 (1980), 21.

8. William Axinn and Arland Thorton, "The Relationship Between Cohabitation and Divorce: Selectivity or Casual Influence?" *Demography,* 29 (1992), 358.

9. Jan E. Stets, "Cohabiting and Marital Aggression: The Role of Isolation," *Journal of Marriage and the Family,* 53 (1991), 669–70.

10. Robert Coombs, "Marital Status and Personal Well-Being: A Literature Review," *Family Relations,* 40 (1991), 97–102.

11. Lee Robins and Darrel Regier, *Psychiatric Disorders in America: The Epidemiologic Catchment Area Study* (New York: Free Press, 1991), 72.

12. Catherine K. Reissman and Naomi Gerstel, "Marital Dissolution and Health: Do Males or Females Have Greater Risk?" *Social Science and Medicine,* 20 (1985), 627.

13. U.S. Department of Justice, Office of Justice Programs, Bureau of Justice Statistics, "Criminal Victimization in the United States, 1992," NCJ–145125, March 1994, 31.

14. Sara McLanahan and Gary Sandefur, *Growing Up With a Single Parent* (Cambridge: Harvard University Press, 1994), 1.

15. Ibid., 2.

16. *Family in America,* February 2000, 2.

17. George Rekers, "Research on the Essential Characteristics of the Father's Role for Family Well-Being," testimony before the Select Committee on Children, Youth and Families, U.S. House of

Representatives, 99th Congress, 2nd session, 25 February 1986, 59–60.

18. *Business Daily,* 12 November 1997.

19. Mike McManus, "Heritage Foundation Calls for Political Leadership on Marriage," *Ethics & Religion,* 22 June 2000, column 982.

20. David Popenoe, "The Controversial Truth," *New York Times,* 26 December 1992, A–21.

21. Frank F. Furstenberg Jr., "History and Current Status of Divorce in the United States," *The Future of Children,* 4, no. 1 (Spring 1994), 37.

22. David Blankenhorn, *Fatherless America: Confronting Our Most Urgent Social Problem* (New York: Basic Books, 1995), 307.

23. James Egan, "When Fathers Are Absent," address given at the National Summit on Fatherhood, sponsored by the National Fatherhood Initiative: Dallas, 27 October 1994.

24. "How Kids Mourn," *Newsweek,* 22 September 1997, 58.

25. See the major work on this by Judith Wallerstein, *The Unexpected Legacy of Divorce* (New York: Hyperion, 2000).

26. Linda Waite and Maggie Gallagher, *The Case for Marriage: Why Married People Are Happier, Healthier and Better Off Financially.*

27. Betsy Hart, "Both Sexes Thrive in Marriage," Scripps Howard News Service, 6 October 2000.

28. Barna Report, 26 April 2000, number 1.

29. T. Suzanne Eller, *Chicken Soup for the Couple's Soul* (Deerfield Beach, Fla.: Health Communications, 1999). Used by permission of the author.

CHAPTER 7

1. Bettina Arndt, "Cohabitors: The New Breed," *The Age*, 7 December 1999.

2. Suzanne Daley, "French Couples Take Plunge That Falls Short of Marriage," *New York Times*, 18 April 2000, 1A.

3. Debra Gaskill, "Shacking Up Strikes Out," *Kettering–Oakwood Times*, Dayton, Ohio, 2 May 2000.

4. Karen Peterson, "Wedded to Relationship but Not to Marriage," *USA Today*, 18 April 2000.

5. David Popenoe, "Cohabitation: The Marriage Enemy," *USA Today*, 28 July 2000.

6. Brian Holman, "Co-habiting First May not Improve Marriage," Scripps Howard Foundation Wire, 5 August 2000.

7. CMFCE@smarriages.com.

8. "Living Together: Facts, Myths, About 'Living in Sin,'" Ann Arbor, 4 February 2000.

9. Murray Dubin, "A Mission to Remedy Marriage," *Philadelphia Inquirer*, 6 August 2000.

10. Larissa Phillips, "The Case Against Matrimony." This article first appeared in Salon.com, at http.//www.salon.com. An on-line version remains in the Salon archives. Reprinted with permission.

11. This is the only time "Israel" occurs in the Song. Its presence is an indication that the poem dates prior to the death of Solomon in 931 B.C. See Carr, *The Song of Solomon*, 110.

12. Nelson, *The Book of Romance*, 76.

13. Carr, 111.

14. Kathy Kristof, "Love and Marriage and Money," *L.A. Times*, 14 September 2000.

15. Garrett, *Proverbs, Ecclesiastes, Song of Solomon*, 402.

16. Dennis Rigstad, "Is It Love or Lust?" *Psychology for Living*, February 1988.

17. *Manhattan Institutes City Journal*, summer 1999.

18. Snaith, *Song of Songs*, 57.

19. Melissa King, "Marriage Vows Renewed by the Pattersons and 1,100 Others at Southeastern Seminary," *Baptist Press*, 20 April 2000.

CHAPTER 8

1. Peggy Fletcher Stack, "What They Didn't Teach You About Sex in Sunday School," *RNS*, 13 October 2000.

2. Nelson, 89.

3. Carin Rubenstein, "The Modern Art of Courtly Love," *Psychology Today*, July 1983, 49.

4. Snaith, *Song of Songs*, 61.

5. Garrett, *Proverbs, Ecclesiastes, Song of Solomon*, 405.

6. Cited in Patterson, *Song of Solomon*, 73.

7. Patricia Dalton, "Daughters of the Revolution," *Washington Post*, 21 May 2000.

8. "What Happy Couples Say About Sex" *Readers' Digest* (February 1989), 13–16.

9. Julie Walsh, "Who's Lighting the Fire?" *WebMD Medical News*, 16 March 2000.

10. Glickman, *A Song for Lovers*, 25.

11. Linda Dillow and Lorraine Pintus, *Intimate Issues* (Colorado Springs: Waterbrook, 1999), 17.

12. Ibid., 19.

CHAPTER 9

1. *London Observer,* 9 January 2000.

2. *World Magazine,* 27 February 1999.

3. *Newsweek,* 1 January 2000.

4. *Cosmopolitan,* January 2000.

5. *South China Post,* 16 November 1999.

6. Bob Turnbull, "What Your Wife Really Needs," *Marriage Partnership* (Fall 1999).

7. Yvonne Turnbull, "What Your Husband Really Wants," *Marriage Partnership* (Fall 1999).

8. Herbert Stein, "Why a Man Needs a Woman," *Readers' Digest* (December 1999).

9. Douglas Wilson, *Reforming Marriage* (Moscow, Idaho: Canon, 1995), 109–10.

CHAPTER 10

1. Abby Ellin, "A Class Feminists Might Abhor," *New York Times,* 5 March 2000.

2. A superb work which looks at the needs of men and women in a similar fashion is Willard F. Harley Jr., *His Needs Her Needs* (Grand Rapids: Revell, 1986). This book has greatly impacted my own thinking, and much of its contents are reflected in this chapter.

3. See also Steven Nock, "Does It Pay for Men in America to Marry and Raise Children?" *Insight,* 29 May 2000, 40–43.

4. Glickman, *A Song for Lovers,* 66.

5. Sandra Aldrich, "Husbands Don't Have Scriptwriters." *Today's Christian Woman* 20.2 (Mar/Apr 1998), 36–39.

6. Gwen Yount Carden, *Dallas Times Herald,* 11 November 1989, 1E.

7. Cecelia Goodnow, "Phil McGraw Draws Raves for 'No Bull' Approach to Rescuing Relationships," *Seattle-Post,* 4 March 2000.

8. Peter Marin, "A Revolution's Broken Promises," *Psychology Today,* July 1983, 55.

9. Stephanie Dunnewind, "It's Time for a New Strategy When Nagging Doesn't Work," *Seattle Times,* 6 April 2000.

10. *Today's Christian Woman,* March-April 1997, 19.

11. Julie Macken, "The Mystery of Why Women Marry," *Financial Review,* 28 August 1999.

12. Kristen Kauffman, "Divorced After Decades," *The Dallas Morning News,* 15 September 2000.

13. *Christianity Today,* 7 February 2000, 55.

14. Carlin Rubenstein, "The Modern Art of Courtly Love," *Psychology Today* (July 1983), 46.

15. *New Man* (September 1997), 20.

16. *Men in Action* (April 1995).

17. Gregory McNamee, quoted in *Reader's Digest* (May 2000), 87.

CHAPTER 11

1. Garrett, *Proverbs, Ecclesiastes, Song of Solomon,* 419.

2. Carr, *The Song of Solomon,* 156.

3. "Snapshots," *USA Today,* 9 June 1998, D1.

4. Dillow and Pintus, *Intimate Issues,* 60.

5. Ibid. See Lisa Douglass, "Orgasms: The Science," *New Woman* (June 1998), 126.

6. Snaith, *Song of Songs,* 100.

7. Carr, 156.

8. Carr, 157; Snaith, 101.

9. Snaith, 103.

10. Garrett, 422.

11. "Keeping the Romance Alive," *Style* (January-February 2000).

12. Carr (162–63) points out that breath could be a reference, in the Hebrew text, to the nipples of her breasts.

13. Terri Lackey, "Counselor Offers Help to Couples for Reclaiming Marriage Intimacy," Baptist Press, 1 November 2000.

14. Garrett, 423–24.

15. "Keeping the Romance Alive."

16. Patterson, *Song of Solomon,* 110.

CHAPTER 12

1. Sue Ellin Browder, "New Rules for a Happy Marriage," *Readers Digest* (November 1999), 100–04.

2. Ginny Graves, "7 Solutions for Sexual Problems," *Readers' Digest* (August 1999), 102–06.

3. Carr, *The Song of Solomon,* 165.

4. David Derbyshire, "A Little Loving Makes the Heart Last Longer," *Sex and Health,* 29 November 2000. *The Telegraph,* #2014.

5. Karen S. Peterson, "Take Time to Nurture a Marriage," *USA Today,* 5 July 2000.

6. Garrett, *Proverbs, Ecclesiastes, Song of Solomon,* 424.

7. Ronald Kotulak, "Lonely Hearts Often Have Sick Hearts," *Chicago Tribune,* 8 August 2000.

8. Glickman, *A Song for Lovers,* 90.

9. Carr, 167.

10. Ibid.

11. Garrett, 425.

12. Michelle Weiner-Davis, "When He's Not in the Mood," *Parade Magazine,* 19 March 2000.

13. Quoted in *Washington Post* Online Edition, 12 November 1999.

14. Adapted from Marie Pierson, "Nourishing Your Love," *Virtue* (date unknown).

15. Quoted from Robert Michael, John Gagnon, Edward Laumann, and Gina Kolata, *Sex in America: A Definitive Study* (New York: Little Brown and Co., 1994).

CHAPTER 13

1. Frederica Matthews-Green, "Men Behaving Justly," *Christianity Today,* 17 November 1997, 45.

2. Glickman, *A Song for Lovers,* 96.

3. Garrett, *Proverbs, Ecclesiastes, Song of Solomon,* 426.

4. Karen S. Petersen, "Quick Lessons for a Long Marriage," *USA Today,* 3 July 2000.

5. Ibid.

6. Barbara DeAngelis, "Are You Too Tired for Sex?," *Family Circle,* 16 October 1990, 32–37.

7. Adapted from John Gottman and Nan Silver, *The Seven Principles for Making Marriage Work* (New York: Crown, 1999).

8. Carr, *The Song of Solomon,* 170.

9. Garrett, 426.

10. Ibid.

11. Patterson, *Song of Solomon,* 117.

12. "Deconstructing the Myths of Marriage," *The London Times,* 2 December 1999.

13. Carr, 171.

14. Jason Millstein, "A Vow of Hard Work," *The Spokesman Review,* 6 March 2000.

15. David Sanford, "Learning to Love Means Staying When You Want to Leave," *Marriage Support* on-line newsletter #681, *Couples Place* Web site. Accessed 28 December 1999.

16. Glickman, 101.

17. Laura Schlessinger, "Modern Women Get No Respect," *The Washington Times.* National Weekly Edition, 23–29 August 1999, 27.

18. Quoted in *World Magazine,* 20 May 1999, 12.

19. "The Truth About In-laws, Reasons for Marrying and Sex, Fidelity and Children." *Town and Country Magazine,* 21 January 1999.

20. From an article by Howard Hendricks, "Yardsticks for Love."

OUR MARRIAGE COVENANT

1. John McNally, "Darling, Will You Spend the Next Six to Ten Years with Me?" *The Onion* Web Site. Accessed 27 December 2000.

2. Eve Tushnet, "New on Fox: I Want a Divorce," *National Catholic Register,* 19 November 2000.